Christian Theology and Scientific Culture

Christian Theology and Scientific Culture

By

THOMAS F. TORRANCE

New York
Oxford University Press
1981

Copyright © 1981 Christian Journals Ltd.

Library of Congress Cataloging in Publication Data

Torrance, Thomas Forsyth, 1913-
  Christian theology and scientific culture.

  (Theology and scientific culture ; 1)
  Bibliography: p.
  Includes index.
  Contents: Christianity in scientific change—The priority of belief—The theology of light—Word and number.
  1. Religion and science—1946- —Addresses, essays, lectures. I. Title. II. Series.
  BL241.T67   1981   261.5'5   81-16780
  ISBN 0-19-520272-4   AACR2

Printing (last digit): 987654321
Printed in Great Britain

Contents

To

James I. McCord

President, Princeton Theological Seminary

and

President, World Alliance of Reformed Churches

in

gratitude and affection

Preface

In several of his brief essays on science and religion Albert Enstein spoke of the strong reciprocal relations and dependencies between them. He discounted the one-sided contrast between knowledge and belief and the claim that belief should be replaced increasingly by knowledge, for that would undermine the enterprise of science itself as well as the conduct of our daily life. The aim of natural science is limited, to determine how facts are related to, and conditioned by, each other, and in that way to attempt what he called 'the posterior reconstruction of existence by the process of conceptualisation'. Science is quite unable through demonstration of this kind to provide the basic belief in the objective rationality of the universe or the aspiration toward truth and understanding which it clearly requires. Without profound faith of this kind, which comes from religion and revelation, science would be inconceivable. However, science itself has a religious dimension in which it contributes toward 'a religious spiritualisation of our understanding of life', if only through the 'humble attitude of mind toward the grandeur of reason incarnate in existence'. Thus religion, for its part, is dependent on the activity of science, for as it makes manifest something of the objective rationality inherent in the universe science helps to purge it of 'the dross of its anthropomorphism'.

The anthropomorphism of which Einstein spoke was of a rather crude sort which any rigorous theology ought to be able to dispose of quite easily. There is, of course, a significant element of anthropomorphism deriving from the profound reciprocity that God establishes with us through his Word which, as Martin Buber used to point out, genuine religious faith cannot do without. It is here, I believe, that the twin Christian doctrines of the Incarnation of the Word of God and the Communion of the Holy Spirit teach us what we may and what we may not 'read back' into God from the relations he sets up between himself and us in this world. On the other hand, there is a subtle abstract form of anthropomorphism found in the projection of idealised creaturely concepts into God, of which liberal theology is particularly and constantly guilty through its development of the autonomous human reason, which is not easy to purge out, but it is here that constant dialogue between theological and natural science can play a very important and helpful role.

It is towards the encouragement of that kind of dialogue that this book is offered, in the hope that it may help people who are interested in natural science as well as those interested in Christian theology. What is intended here is not that theology should take into its material content ideas that derive from natural scientific knowledge of the universe, any more than natural science should incorporate into its developing stock of ideas distinctly theological conceptions. That would be both unscientific and untheological, and could only bring theology and science into useless conflict with one another. What is envisaged here is an exercise in conjoint thinking where theological science and natural science have common ground within the rationalities and objectivities of the created order but where they each pursue a different objective. So far as theology is concerned, the claim is advanced that theology cannot be pursued in any proper and rigorous way in detachment from the determinate framework of the spatio-temporal universe within which God addresses his Word to us and calls us to know and love and serve him. It is, I believe, indifference to that framework of objective rationality, or the isolation of theology from natural science, that lies behind the sense of lostness and bewilderment, as well as the sloppiness and ambiguity of thought, so often manifest in contemporary theological literature. On the other hand, it is through taking that framework seriously that we are enabled to hear the Word of God in such an objective way that we do not confuse it with the creaturely things we tell ourselves about one another and are tempted to project into God. It is through deep-going dialogue with science and submission of our own theological conceptions to the critical questions it addresses to us that we are helped to purge our minds of pseudo-theological as well as pseudo-scientific notions, and so are enabled to build up theological knowledge in a positive way on its own proper ground: God's self-revelation and self-communication to us in the incarnation of his eternal Word in Jesus Christ.

Apart from the second chapter on 'The Priority of Belief', this book comprises in an extended form *The Queen's University Lectures in Theology,* to be delivered in Belfast in October 1980. It represents the first in a series of books to be published in the next few years under the aegis of *The Templeton Foundation* and with the general title of *Theology and Scientific Culture*. Publication will take place on both sides of the Atlantic, and in French and German as well as in English. In this venture scientists and theologians (some of whom are both scientists and theologians) from various countries hope to share their thought in clarifying the interrelations of science and theology, with the aim of providing a platform for deeper understanding and wider cooperation between them.

I should like to express the appreciation of all concerned to the Rev. Wilbert Forker, Vice-President of *The Templeton Foundation,* who initiated and now manages this exciting project. My own debt to him for his unceasing encouragement and kindness is more than can be expressed in a few words.

Once more I am deeply and happily indebted to my son, the Rev. Dr. Iain Torrance, for many helpful comments and his assistance with the proofs.

Canty Bay,
East Lothian

September 10, 1980

Thomas F. Torrance

1.

Christianity in Scientific Change

Last year we commemorated two events of great significance in the history of natural science, which took place a hundred years earlier in 1879, the death of James Clerk Maxwell and the birth of Albert Einstein. We were reminded of another year of similar significance, 1642, which saw both the death of Galileo Galilei and the birth of Isaac Newton, the two giants who between them decisively turned the course of scientific thought in developing the method and structure of classical mechanics applicable to all motion in the universe. With the work of Clerk Maxwell and Einstein, however, there took place an even more basic change in the understanding of physical reality and its scientific explanation which has altered the fundamental structure of physics. Clerk Maxwell stands for the discovery of the mathematical properties of radiation through which the understanding of electricity, magnetism and light were brought into a coherent, unified conceptual framework. The physical and mathematical insights which this embodied were not only a great intellectual achievement in themselves, but in the form of Maxwell's partial differential equations have proved to be immensely fertile in subsequent science leading up to Einstein and beyond, for they are, as Einstein claimed, the natural expression of the primary realities of physics. Einstein himself was responsible for the greatest achievement of all in his formulation of the special and general theories of relativity, which irreversibly switched the course of classical physics and laid it securely upon profounder, unifying foundations appropriate to a much wider range of empirical evidence — all beginning from his startling papers of 1905 on quantum theory, statistical mechanics and special relativity. The technical results flowing from Clerk Maxwell's discoveries are to be seen everywhere to-day, in our systems of illumination, locomotion and communication, and their application to modern industry and life, but the deep change from mechanical to relational thinking which he initiated reached its culmination in Einstein's work. The effect of Einstein's discoveries reaches down into the very foundations of our understanding of the universe, affecting everything we know far beyond the limits of physics. Thus the combined work of Clerk Maxwell and Albert Einstein imports a radical alteration in the regulative basis of knowledge, transforming not only the structure of science but our basic ways of knowing.

I do not propose to discuss how these changes came about or the lines of interconnection between Maxwellian and Einsteinian physics, or what all this means for classical Newtonian science. What I propose to do is to offer some kind of answer to the question: How are we, from within the Christian faith, to regard these changes that have been taking place, and what is their significance for Christianity to-day?

Let us pause here to note the importance of this question, for it has to do with the immense impact of science upon human culture, in the way we think and behave. Whether we like it or not theology is always inextricably involved in culture, past or on-going, if only because theology must use language, and language is rooted in society and the physical universe of space and time in which we live. Let us not forget that much of our basic knowledge on which we rely throughout our life is gained in our earliest years, as we learn to speak and adapt ourselves to the physical and social world around us. A child by the age of five, for example, has learned more 'physics' than he could ever bring to explicit understanding and expression even if he turned out to be a very brilliant physicist. We always know more than we can tell, and our implicit thinking is shaped by the world of knowledge embedded in and handed on in the tradition of culture into which we are born. It is in reliance upon that implicit understanding and knowing that all our explicit thought and formulation, and all genuine advance, take place in any science, physical, social or theological. This does not imply that we must operate uncritically within the knowledge or wisdom accumulated in our cultural tradition, just because we are unable to extricate ourselves from involvement in it. On the contrary, it is because our thought is so powerfully influenced by culture that we must bring its latent assumptions out into the open and put them to the test. Cultural assumptions, after all, are most dangerous when we are unaware of them.

No more than any other science can theology be indifferent to its cultural tradition and milieu if it really is to be theology. In so far as theology is influenced by culture it will, wittingly or unwittingly, reflect culture and use it as a medium or sounding-board for its message. Of course if it merely reflects a culture, then the cultural medium takes over and the medium becomes the message, and theology in any proper sense becomes submerged. Hence if theology is not to be swamped by cultural relativism but is to retain its integrity, it must put all cultural assumptions rigorously to the test before the compelling claims of its own proper subject-matter and its objective evidential grounds. On the other hand, it must not be forgotten that theology may have far-reaching effects upon human culture. Where has that been more evident than in the immense influence of Augustinian theology upon all aspects of our Western culture for nearly a millennium and a half?

Our concern here, however, is not just with the tradition of human culture which many peole still regard as limited to the arts and humanities, but with *scientific culture* which must surely be recognised as having the most powerful and wide-spread impact in modern times. It is indeed a *culture* of the greatest significance: not to be influenced by it is really to be something of a barbarian! Here too Christian theology has been heavily implicated from the start, both for good and for evil. Thus through the concept of radical contingence, derived from reflection on the inter-relation of the incarnation and the creation, Christian theology has contributed in a staggering way to the very foundations of empirical science, as we realise more and more to-day in the disclosure of its under-lying assumptions. Yet it is to theology also, in the fateful combination of the notions of immutability and unmoved mover applied to the doctrine of God, that we must trace back the idea of inertia or of an inertial system which lies behind the conception of a closed mechanistic universe that has so severely constricted the human spirit. It is then in the context of scientific culture that the question we have raised has its crucial importance, for it is within this context that Christian belief and Christian theology have to articulate and express themselves. Moreover, as in the early centuries of our era so to-day Christianity must contribute creatively to the controlling ideas of this scientific culture if it is to take deeper root and grow within it. I do not believe that this will be possible unless Christian theology is prepared to engage in radical and critical clarification of its own conceptual tradition in the light of questions arising from its interaction with scientific developments, as well as in deep-level testing of the preconceptions and beliefs underlying these developments.

Let me single out at this point, then, several of the major problems which have arisen in the course of natural science since Galileo and Newton calling for paradigmatic change in its structure and enterprise, and consider them from within the perspective of the Christian faith.

(1) The conception of the universe as a closed and rigidly mechanical system. This arose out of a way of thinking of the universe as consisting ultimately of bodies in motion interacting causally and externally on one another, when Galileo abstracted from the natural cohesion of things those features of nature — the so-called 'primary qualities' — which are quantifiable as the proper subject-matter for scientific attention. Since they alone, he held, are open to mathematical representation and are as such capable of complete formalisation, it is by taking them only into account that an exact mechanical explanation of things in the world may be given. The identification of this way of thinking with 'the scientific outlook' reached its dominance in European culture with Pièrre Simon de Laplace at the end of the eighteenth and in the early part of the nineteenth century.

In accordance with this view science proceeds analytically and atomistically, by breaking nature down into minute particles and explaining everything in terms of the causal laws of physics and chemistry. Laplace claimed, therefore, that since everything, animate or inanimate, can be explained in terms of the specifiable elements which compose it, it should be possible from a knowledge of the exact position and momentum of every particle of matter in the universe to compute, in accordance with the laws of motion, all past and future states of affairs in it, that is, to gain a complete understanding of the universe from an exact knowledge of all atomic data. And that Laplace held to be the rigorous ideal of all natural science. This thoroughly reductionist and determinist concept of universal knowledge presupposes, of course, that the whole of nature is nothing but a vast machine. The logical deficiency of this view, as Michael Polanyi has argued so clearly, becomes manifest as soon as it is realised that any machine with which we are familiar embodies operational principles that are simply not explainable in terms of the laws of physics and chemistry that govern its component particulars—that is why we need sciences of engineering over and above the sciences of physics and chemistry. This argument applies with even greater force to the 'machine-like' operational principles of biological organisms. However, the utter absurdity of a rigidly determinist and mechanistic explanation is most evident whenever it is applied to man himself, for it fails to account for his distinctive nature as a personal, rational agent, and is incapable of answering the really important questions which he is bound to raise. All our mathematico-mechanical formalisations are meaningless unless they bear upon non-mathematical and non-mechanical experience and reality. That is why any Laplacian account of the universe, or of natural science itself, solely in terms of impersonal formalisations in which the mind itself is missing, is and must be inevitably rejected by the human spirit, for in such a closed, determinist and mechanistic conception of things the human spirit has no place and no room is left for all his higher pursuits in the arts and humanities or in religion.

So far as the development of scientific culture is concerned, what was ultimately at stake in the Laplacian world view was the basic understanding of the real world and the very nature of empirico-theoretical science: through a rather disastrous misunderstanding it became trapped in an impasse. That first began to be recognised with the break-down of a mechanical explanation of the electromagnetic field. For all his brillaint achievements in his attempt to offer an interpretation of the phenomena of radiation along the lines of Newtonian mechanics, Clerk Maxwell himself insisted that explanation along these lines was finally 'unworkable', and offered instead a relational mode of interpretation and explanation without recourse to Newtonian mechanics. That was the beginning of the end of the mechanistic conception of the universe, but it took some time for it to mature to the point we have now reached in the open-structured universe of general relativity and non-equilibrium thermodynamics. Along with this there has come a realisation of the abstract and artificial character of the classical (Galilean and Newtonian) notions of causality and mechanical relation, and therefore of the limitations not only of a strictly instrumentalist scientific method as it had hitherto been conceived but of the scientific enterprise as such, for even the physical world has been found to be more subtle and flexible in its order and more resistant to our abstract formalisations than we had come to believe.

The decisive switch from a totally mechanistic conception of the universe and the imperialistic scientism that went with it certainly represents a change that is very welcome to the Christian faith, if only because that way of thinking axiomatically ruled out *ab initio* any thought of living interaction between God and the world he has made. The liberation of the human spirit from a closed determinist continuum of cause and effect, which is now taking place, makes for the resuscitation of belief in divine providence and divine response to human prayer, but so far as specific Christian faith is concerned it allows the basic doctrines of the incarnation and resurrection to be thought out and formulated on their own proper ground without extraneous conditions unscientifically imposed under the absurd claims of a completely formalised model of the universe.

(2)   The container notion of time and space. This is an idea with which we seem to be naturally familiar since we regularly speak of things or events as *in* time or *in* space, as if time and space were receptacles or boxes of some sort containing material objects. Although the ultimate origin of this notion is to be traced back to early Greek philosophy and science, as well as the more sophisticated concepts of Plato, Aristotle and the Stoics, it was given a new lease of life after the Renaissance and built into the fabric of Western science. Two forms of this container notion of time and space have had a powerful impact upon scientific developments: (a) the Newtonian and (b) the Kantian.

(a)   With Newton time and space were identified with the all-comprehending mind and immanent presence of God, the infinite receptacle containing and imposing order on all creaturely beings. He spoke of this as absolute mathematical time and space in contrast to relative apparent time and space which characterise the phenomenal world of bodies in motion. It was important for Newton's theoretic system of the world that time and space should constitute an isotropic, necessary and unchanging frame of reference for the orderly reduction of all bodies in motion to

patterns which were amenable to mathematico-
mechanical calculation and to formalisation in
immutable laws. He achieved that by relating time and
space not only to the eternity and infinity of God but to
his immutability and impassibility, which allowed him
to think of absolute time and space as containing all
bodies in the universe and controlling their behaviour
without being changed in themselves by what they
contained and controlled — that is what he meant by
the term 'absolute'. Time and space thus identified
with the unchanging presence and reality of God
constituted an independent cause or inertial system in
the whole geometrico-causal structure of Newtonian
physics and mechanics.

We have already noted the problematic character of
the scientific world view to which it gave rise, in the
mechanistic conception of the universe, and we shall
later have to consider the damaging dualism which the
concept of independent and absolute time and space
imported into scientific culture, but at this point let us
note the bearing it has upon the idea of incarnation.
Newton himself saw the problem very clearly when he
asked how we can think of God who is the infinite
container of all things as himself becoming man, and
so one of the bodies in motion contained by him. He
claimed that God could no more be thought of as
becoming incarnate than we can think of a pail as
becoming one of the things it contains, and so Newton
openly threw in his lot with the heretic Arius rather
than with Athanasius and the Nicene Creed. Actually
Athanasius had already seen that the Christian message
of the incarnation of God in Jesus Christ conflicted
sharply with the container notions of space that
prevailed in the world of Greek culture in his own time.
He was prompted to rethink radically the whole concept
of the relation of God to the space and time of the

world which he had made out of nothing, and in this way contributed so powerfully to the reconstruction of the foundations of ancient philosophy and science in the early Christian centuries.

(b)   With the so-called 'Copernican revolution' of Immanuel Kant the concept of absolute time and space was transferred from the mind of God to the mind of man. Newton's way of relating absolute time and space to the comprehending and controlling mind of God had the effect of reinforcing the basic conviction of science that we are in contact with a world of objective rational order which exists independently of our knowing of it, but the effect of Kant's identification of time and space with built-in capacities or *a priori* forms of intuition was very different: it undermined the concept of objectivity in its classical form and called in question the independent reality of the world apart from the modes of its appearance to us. Kant held that we can know things only as we shape them for ourselves through the structures of our consciousness which are absolute and unchanging, for they are not affected by what we know or seek to grasp with our minds. That is to say, an objectifying mode of thought is substituted for a genuinely objective mode of thought: we cannot know things as they are in themselves or in their internal relations but only in terms of the orderly patterns we impose upon them. Quite consistently, therefore, Kant claimed that the human intellect does not draw its laws out of nature but reads them into nature.

Since substance and causality were also regarded as in-built categories of the understanding, Kant's object-ifying way of thought had the effect of generalising into a universal dogma the determinism latent in the Newtonian outlook upon the mechanistic universe. If the human mind reads its laws into nature in accordance with the unchanging structures of its intuition and understanding it cannot help doing so! A necessitarianism of this kind leaves no room for contingence or contingent intelligibility in nature and so cuts away the foundation for a genuinely empirical science. At the same time, if we cannot know things as they are in themselves or in their internal relations, then it is not surprising if it should be claimed that scientific theories and laws have no bearing upon being or reality independent of ourselves, but have to be regarded as no more than 'mental artifices' or 'mental fictions' which we have constructed for our convenience. That was how Ernst Mach and the positivists found they had to assess the discoveries and formulations of natural science, even to the extent of challenging the existence of atoms in a remarkable controversy with Max Planck!

The Kantian denial of knowledge of things in themselves and restriction of knowledge only to things as they appear to us has far-reaching implications, not only for scientific culture. So far as God is concerned it means that God is and must remain quite unknowable beyond all intuitive representations, for he cannot be thought of as falling under the power of man's objectifying operations, shaped by the active reason and held under its control like the phenomenal realities of our this-worldly experience. So far as Jesus Christ is concerned, it means that all knowledge of Jesus Christ in himself must be ruled out of account as mere pretence, for all that may be known of him derives from his appearance to his contemporaries or rather from what they made of his appearance for themselves; but in the nature of the case what they made of Jesus' appearance for themselves is not something which can be known in itself, for we can do no more than claim to know what we can shape for ourselves out of their objectifying operations, That is the devastating effect that Kant's inversion of the Newtonian mode of scientific knowing has had on so much New Testament scholarship in modern times. Combined with Newton's denial of the possibility of incarnation it goes far to explain the distorting presuppositions that lie behind Bultmann's demythologising programme.

So far as basic scientific developments are concerned, however, the ground for that way of thinking has been removed, with the shattering not only of the container notion of time and space but of the whole concept of independent or absolute time and space (and thus of an inertial system) whether in its Newtonian or in its Kantian form, for now time and space are found to be objective, covariant features of on-going empirical reality. When with Clerk Maxwell a rigidly mechanical way of thinking began to give place to a dynamic and relational way of thinking, new kinds of questions had to be asked which gave rise to a corresponding change in notions of time and space. These were questions as to the actual web of relations in which things are found, which yielded the view that the whole of physical reality could be represented as a field whose components depend on four space-time parameters, as Einstein has expressed it. The switch to this way of thinking has not been taking place without a severe struggle in dismantling the highly questionable and static structures of thought derived from the Newtonian and Laplacian outlooks, and is still being completed as the vast implications of general relativity for our understanding of the universe are steadily being worked out. What is clear already is that a dynamic and relational concept of space and time has entrenched itself in the very foundations of our scientific understanding in such a way as finally to eliminate the old container notions and to expose all the fallacies that derived from them.

From the perspective of the Christian faith, the immediate upshot of these developments is the raising of questions for biblical interpretation and theological formulation which have the uncomfortable effect of putting them to the test and exposing any entanglement with unwarranted presuppositions and transient frames of thought which bear little objective relation to their distinctive subject-matter. On the other hand, the collapse of the objectifying programme of knowledge before the recovery of ontology in our understanding of physical law, opens the way for a realist reconstruction of theology parallel to and in interaction with the realist reconstruction that has been taking place in the foundations of pure science. One great benefit accruing from this will undoubtedly be a profounder grasp of the created or contingent order within which both natural and theological science have to operate and to co-operate in fidelity to the nature of the universe that God has made.

(3) The dualism between theoretical and empirical aspects of reality. Here modern science has had to wrestle with what is in some respects the most deeply entrenched and inveterate difficulty in traditional science, which underlies the problematic features we have been considering. The roots of this dualism go back to the ancient Hellenic dichotomy between the intelligible and sensible realms which had been taken up and made paradigmatic by the great Augustinian tradition in Western thought and culture. With the rise of modern science this was given a new form in the radical dictinction between the geometric frame and the phenomenal surface of experience which was developed in different but coordinate ways by Galileo and Descartes. At the same time, of course, modern science insisted on bringing together — and this was one of its distinctive features — theory and experiment, and

did so in such a way that it set scientific inquiry on the road of its remarkable advances. It was with Newton above all that theory and experiment were combined in this fertile way, but it was also through Newton that the dualism between the theoretical and empirical aspects of reality was mathematically elaborated and systematically built into the structure of classical physics, in his insistence on clamping down upon the world of contingent events the rigid isotropic framework of absolute mathematical time and space, which, precisely in order to achieve the uniformity in scientific formalisation he wanted, had to be kept independent of and unaffected by empirical reality, as an inertial system. It is due to that paradox in the heart of Newtonian physics that there has been such a struggle to overcome the dualism posited by absolute time and space. Newton's way of coordinating mathematical time and space and apparent time and space proved immensely successful within the parameters of Euclidean geometry and at certain levels of experience, but it gave rise to the grave problems we have already noted and, as Einstein has shown, it lay at the source of the discrepancies steadily emerging in scientific theories. Newton's error lay in separating experience from geometry and then in crushing an understanding of the universe of bodies in motion within the framework of an idealised geometry concerned with the relations between rigid bodies independent of time. That is, physical knowledge of the real world was interpreted and formalised in terms of an antecedently and independently conceived theoretic framework which artificially gave it an abstract determinist pattern. Hence Einstein called for an indissoluble integration of geometry and experience at all levels of scientific investigation and theoretical formulation. Geometry must be brought into the midst of physical knowledge of the empirical world of space and time where it would be four-dimensional. This integration of the geometrical and the physical or of the theoretical and empirical entailed a unity of form and being or of structure and matter, which had far-reaching implications for fundamental knowledge in every sphere of human inquiry. Expressed more generally, it involved the unification of epistemology and ontology in rigorous fidelity to the fact that theoretical and empirical factors are found already inhering in one another in objective reality.

Strenuous exertions were required of natural science in order to achieve that result, but in the meantime the epistemological dualism that derived from Galilean and Newtonian thought proved particularly damaging because it was consistently worked out and built into the fabric of a scientific culture which increasingly provided the framework for people's thought. Over wide areas of life and culture the phenomenal level of human experience was torn away from its ontological roots and schematised to the artifically contrived patterns of a mechanically conceived universe. With the loss of the natural coherences which this brought about, human existence and behaviour became deprived of a consistent substructure to hold them meaningfully together, and there set in the disintegration of form, along with a frightening dissolution of meaning, with which we are only too familiar in our fragmented modern culture.

It is in this general context of thought and culture in which a deep-seated epistemological dualism had been at work severing form from being that modern Christianity has found itself having to fight for its existence and integrity, much as early Christianity had to do in the second, third and fourth centuries against the radical dualisms of the Gnostics and Arians which in different ways threatened the very core of the Christian Gospel and sought to substitute some sort of contrived mythology for a realistic theology of the incarnation and creation. That struggle still continues, for unfortunately dualist habits of thought left behind in the advance of the pure sciences are still rampant in general and popular scientific culture, where they represent an anachronistic hang-over from the nineteenth century and easily snare the unselfcritical scholar or undisciplined theologian. The damaging effect of this dualism is widely apparent to-day in two related ways: (a) in detaching Christ from God and (b) in detaching Christianity from Christ. The detachment of Jesus Christ from oneness with God robs him of any central or ultimate place in the Christian faith, for what is then important is not the person of Christ himself but the ideas he mediates about God and humanity. There inevitably follows from this a detachment of Christianity from Christ who is relegated to only transient second-order significance and the attachment of Christianity to the Church regarded as an ecclesiastical institution competing with the technological society, which provokes a far from happy reaction from our young people to-day: or there follows the attachment of Christianity to society itself where it becomes secularised as little more than a movement for social righteousness but rapidly suffers from the decomposing patterns of modern social existence and its fragmenting culture.

Serious as this state of affairs is, I believe one must regard it as a transient phenomenon, the sort of thing that is likely to take place in the *time-lag* between any radical change in epistemological foundations, first principles and basic methods, and the working out of its consequences in the more superficial layers of life and thought, since a transitional period of this kind is regularly characterised by not a little in the way of confusion, fudging of issues, hybrid solutions and regressive tendencies under the break-up of customary habits of thought. However, since dualist modes of knowing and interpreting reality have already been overcome through a rigorously scientific unitary understanding of the orderly universe in which theological science as well as natural science must function, a very different outlook is promised. This is one in which an integrating, onto-relational approach operating with a natural fusion of form and being, not a merely analytical, disintegrating approach operating with a divorce of form from being, will be brought to bear on our understanding of Jesus Christ and the Gospel, and of course on the Biblical witness and tradition — a way of thinking which in the fourth century resulted in the Nicene-Constantinopolitan Creed.

In concluding this discussion let me pin-point several positive aspects in recent scientific change which may affect Christian theology beneficially. This is not to claim that they can contribute to the material content of Christian theology but that they can play a healthy role in helping it to clarify its own way of thinking and formulating the truth under the compulsion of God's self-revelation to mankind within the structured objectivities of the universe which are steadily disclosed through scientific inquiry.

(1) A more flexible and yet a more faithful way of knowing appropriate to what we seek to know. In natural science this change has arisen in reciprocal relation to a corresponding change in our understanding of the contingent nature of the universe itself. We know things strictly in accordance with their natures or what they are in themselves and at the same time we

allow what things actually are to reveal themselves to us and thereby to determine for us the content and the form of our knowledge of them. Proper knowing takes place through a steady dynamic interaction between our minds and objective reality. We encourage our thinking to adapt itself to the structural relations and coherent patterns already inherent in nature independent of our knowing of it and so to predominate over any antecedently conceived frames of thought on our part, and thereby we learn more and more to appreciate the contingency, subtlety, richness, variability, and complexity of nature. Thus epistemological and ontological considerations are dynamically wedded in our inquiries and formulations.

According to Einstein this change in scientific thought, which represents a victory over the notions of absolute time and space or over the idea of an inertial system, became possible only because the concept of the material object was gradually replaced as the fundamental concept of physics by that of the field, and the Newtonian way of conceiving of physical laws was replaced by another which equated them with dynamic field-structures. This implied a view of contingent reality as a continuous integrated manifold of fields of force in which relations between bodies are just as ontologically real as the bodies themselves, for it is in their interrelations and transformations that things are found to be what and as and when they are. They are to be investigated and interpreted not by reference to a static uniformity of causal patterns abstracted from the actual fields of force in which they exist, but in accordance with their immanent relatedness in the universe and in terms of their own inherent dynamic order. In such a universe in which form and being and movement are inseparably fused together, things and events are to be explained and interpreted in terms of *ontological reasons.* We must penetrate into what they are in themselves in their own interior relations, in which they exhibit an intrinsic intelligibility independent of our perceiving and conceiving of them, and thereby discriminate themselves from our scientific constructs and formalisations about them and require their constant revision.

The importance of this change in the understanding of rigorous scientific knowledge for Christian theology can hardly be over-estimated, if only because it gives no ground for the mistakes that arise so easily when form and being are held apart and the evidential and conceptual relation between human knowing and God's self-revelation is cut away. On the contrary, in accordance with the scientific principle that everything must be investigated and conceived strictly in ways appropriate to its nature in a process of dynamic interaction between the knower and the known, a different approach is taken up in the interpretative bases of theology. The evangelical sources for our knowledge of Jesus Christ, for example, must be allowed to speak to us in their own right, and Jesus Christ himself must be understood in accordance with his own intrinsic Logos. So long as we operate with an axiomatic disjunction between form and being, we start right away with a discrepancy between his 'image' and his 'reality' and are then thrown back on themselves and our own fantasies to make what sense we can of him for ourselves — i.e. the all too familiar line taken by ancient and modern Arians!

On the other hand, if we operate with a unity of form and being, or the inherence of theoretical and empirical components in one another, then as in every rigorous science we allow the reality into which we are inquiring to prove itself to us, and we must be prepared to commit or refrain from committing ourselves in accordance with what happens. Differences arise, of course, in accordance with the nature of the field or the reality in question, which must be taken into account here, for we cannot begin by assuming that God is to be known in precisely the same way as created or inert realities. In natural science we are concerned, for the most part, with inert material which we seek to know in accordance with what it is in itself: hence we must find ways in which it may be brought to disclose itself to us in reaction to our experimental questions. In theological science, however, we have to do with the living God, the Creator of the universe who maintains it in its orderly existence through unceasing interaction with it, and whom we may know only through his active self-revelation to us within the creation where he has planted us. It is, then, with the relation of Jesus Christ to the active self-disclosure of God that we have to reckon in our theological inquiry. Is that not what we are concerned with when we listen to the Gospel and allow it on its own evidential ground to speak to us in its own right? We begin with the self-identifying movement of Christ as one sent to us out of the love of God, and respond to the summons to understand him out of the coincidence of the image he exhibits toward us and the reality he is in himself — and we find that we have to reckon here with the power of Christ's own presence as the risen Lord, that is with the unity of form and being and movement which he constitutes in himself. He challenges us to know him is such a way that we allow our minds to come under the creative and transforming power of what he is in his self-disclosure as the embodied Word of God. Everything hinges on the question whether he really is in himself what he discloses toward us in his mediation of divine truth, salvation and life, or, to express it the other way round, whether what he is toward us in his mediation of the saving and forgiving power of God he is antecedently and inherently in his own Person. That is the question, to put it succinctly, whether Jesus Christ is *of one being* with God, the familiar *homoousion* which the Nicene fathers found to be the 'king-pin' which holds the Christian faith together, for to sever the ontological bond between Christ and God would empty the Gospel of divine love and forgiveness of its ultimate validity and reality. That is the crucial point where we must be prepared either to commit ourselves or not to the inter-action of God himself with us in Jesus Christ.

(2) The variety and unity of rational order in the creation. General relativity, which defines the universe as a continuous whole, considerably reinforces the conviction deriving from the Christian doctrine of the creation of all things by one God, that the universe is characterised throughout by a unitary rational order. If the universe were not everywhere inherently and harmoniously rational, it would not be open to consistent rational understanding and interpretation. Unless we believed in the reality and intelligibility of the external world there would be no natural science, but neither would there be any natural science if the results of our various inquiries throughout nature failed to harmonise with one another. On the other hand, nature everywhere manifests itself to us in a limitless variety of form and pattern through its pervasive rational order, without which there would be no empirical science deploying experimental forms of inquiry, for everything about the universe would be so uniform and homogeneous that it would be directly accessible to knowledge through logico-deductive processes alone. The unity of form and being implied by general relativity does not mean, as we have seen, the imposition upon contingent reality of some necessitarian isotropic system of form but rather such

an inherence of form in nature that it is affected by its space-time dynamic variations. This requires us to take into our reckoning the fact that the pervasive rational order which we find in the world is multivariable in its modes as well as unitary in its character.

There are, then, distinctive forms of rational order in the universe which require for their understanding and articulation distinctive ways of thought and expression, but far from conflicting with one another they involve and combine with one another in the one rational order of the universe. The basic forms of rational order demanding recognition are the numerical, the verbal, the organic and the aesthetic. Each is rational in its own right but in a distinctive way, so that it would be irrational to schematise it to a different rational form, as happens so frequently in biological science, for example, when the distinctive kind of order manifested by living organisms is reductively converted into numerate order which characterises inanimate determinate matter. In accordance with the principle that different realities are to be investigated and known out of their own natures and internal relations, the distinctive forms of rational order that are disclosed by nature must all be given their full value. Nevertheless, they are all interrelated within the rational harmony of the universe, so that their no less distinctive combinations have to be taken into account in our inquiries if we are not to impose needless limitations and even distortions on whatever may be disclosed to us.

There are two cognate aspects of this variety and unity of rational order which have a particular relevance for theology, not least in its dialogue with natural science.

(a) The first has to do with the fact that we have to develop different languages appropriate to the distinctive kinds of reality we encounter, if we are to understand them adequately and coordinate them in our thought. This is one of the outstanding features of the modern scientific development which has seen the invention of quite new symbolic or technical languages to convey the conceptual structures forced on our thought at different levels of our investigation into the behaviour of things in nature. We have to learn not to confuse these languages, for that can only obstruct our investigations and give rise to serious misunderstanding. Thus, for example, it is important to frame our questions in appropriate language if we are to get appropriate answers. If we ask biological questions we still get only biological, not geometrical, answers, and that is as it should be. Anthropological, psychological, or physico-chemical questions will not yield theological insights for which only theological questions are appropriate. The fact that we have to use a verbal medium, such as English, French or German, in which to articulate these technical languages, brings its own difficulties, for every verbal medium is bound up with a long cultural tradition and is inevitably affected by conceptual habits which may often be inappropriate or misleading. Hence we must purify and refine the technical language if we are to use it for relevant questions. We normally do this by asking questions in a series in such a way that we learn to question our questions in the light of the answers given in order to uncover concealed assumptions or conceptualities affecting the way in which they have been framed, and we keep on doing that so that our questions may be increasingly adapted to the nature of the field in which we are at work in the hope of inducing apposite answers. Confusion is bound to arise when we ask questions in one language about something described in another language, without taking the differences into account and employing some sort of hermeneutical device for translation and adjustment from one language to another. We have an obvious instance of this kind of confusion when the Biblical account of creation in the book of Genesis is correlated in a direct way on one and the same logical level with a natural scientific account of the expansion of the universe and of the evolutionary process within it. The Biblical account and the natural scientific account express different kinds of relation which simply cannot be combined on one and the same level without serious confusion and contradiction. We have a somewhat similar problem in physics when we try to bring together on one and the same logical level accounts of classical-mechanical and of quantum-mechanical relations, which inevitably gives rise to paradoxes and absurdities. We require something like transformation equations enabling us to pass in thought from one kind of relation to the other, while keeping distinct the different languages or accounts used. This kind of passage is not so easy when it comes to the interrelationship between theological discourse and natural scientific discourse, but that makes constant dialogue between the two all the more necessary, if we are to respect the unitary rationality of the created universe.

(b) In the second place, then, we must learn how properly to coordinate different modes of rational order. The need for this is very obvious in biology in which we inquire into complex organic structures integrating matter, energy and life. The relation between matter and living structure involves the coordination of numerate and organismic rational order, but at the same time the distinctive rationality of aesthetic form clearly enters into our understanding of the morphological structures arising out of biological processes. It may well be that topological modes of thought may play a significant role in linking our understanding of matter to that of living structures, but organismic form surely deserves to be considered in its own right, otherwise we would be tempted to lapse into a damaging reductionist explanation of living organisms. Be that as it may, biological science demonstrates the need to coordinate distinct modes of rational order if adequate understanding of living organisms is to be achieved.

Proper combination of different modes of rationality with one another is not less important in Christian theology, if only because in theology we are concerned not simply with relations between man and God but with those relations actualised within the rational structures and real objectivities of the spatio-temporal universe. Theological forms of thought and speech certainly are intended to lift our minds to a realm where they are not tied down to material realities or subjected to their control but are wide open to the infinite objectivity and inexhaustible intelligibility of God the Creator of all things, but they would have no relevance or meaning for us if they were cut adrift from the actualities of the created order through which God reveals himself to us and summons us to respond to him. To a certain extent something similar applies to all formal and symbolic systems whether linguistic, logical or mathematical, for they enable our minds to rise above the world where we may think freely and objectively about it, but they would become vague and useless if they did not retain some authentic and natural coordination with empirical existence. Detachment from ontological reference to reality in any sphere finally renders thought and speech empty and meaningless. In Christian theology, however, where we are concerned with the self-giving and self-communication of God to us in and through the incarnation of his

Word in Jesus Christ, we have to reckon with a profounder dimension of ontological reference, for it is with the objectivity of God the creative source of all rational order that we have to do, confronting us within the created objectivities of our empirical existence which lends those created objectivities an intensity and depth of significance they can have in no other science. This applies to the whole course and sweep of divine revelation to mankind through Israel, in which word-rationality and number-rationality are inseparably co-ordinated with one another, that is, in which God's communication to us through word cannot be severed from the determinate structures of the physical creation to which we belong as human beings.

However, let us think specifically of one particular doctrine which may serve to throw into relief what is involved here, the resurrection of Jesus Christ from the grave. If the resurrection is cut adrift from spatio-temporal structures and objectivities it becomes quite indistinct and amorphous and is easily laid open to mythological fantasising and prevarication. Of course the concept of the resurrection from the dead is quite different from that of the mere resuscitation of a corpse, for here we meet with an immediate act of God creatively transforming a corrupt state of affairs in the tomb, for the resurrected body of Jesus is very different from a body somehow revived but still subject to corruption and mortality. This is a recreative and reordering act of God within the structures and object-ivities of our spatio-temporal existence in the flesh, so that if the resurrection is cut adrift from empirical correlates in time and space, e.g. the emptying of the tomb, it becomes evacuated of rational meaning and is nonsensical; and cannot be connected up coherently with the historical Jesus, let alone with ourselves as human beings in need of salvation in our whole

psycho-physical existence. If at this point the ontological bond between Jesus Christ and the being and
act of God is snapped, as St. Paul argued, we make
God out to be a liar and we are yet in our sins. Moreover
if the resurrection does not involve the empty tomb,
there can be no possibility of coordinating rational
thought and speech about it with basic concepts and
statements arising out of our ordinary life and empirical
knowledge, and therefore no possibility of meaningful
dialogue with natural science which operates and must
operate within the relations of space and time that are
the regular carriers of all rational order.

(3)   The stratified structure of the universe and of
our knowledge of it. It has long been recognised that
an epistemic correlation arises between the knowing
mind and what it seeks faithfully to know, but now in
the advance of the scientific enterprise it has steadily
emerged that in the on-going processes of interaction
with nature a structural kinship develops between the
stratification of scientific knowledge and the stratification of the universe. Scientific knowledge embodies
layers of coherent comprehension which answer to and
are affected by the coordinated layers of orderly
relations in reality itself. This integrated complex
structure in reality and in our corresponding knowledge
of it forms an ascending hierarchy of orderly relations
which prove to be open upward in ever wider compre-
hensiveness and profounder ranges of intelligibility but
which cannot be flattened downward by being reduced
to isomorphic relations on one and the same level. It is
characterised throughout by what might be described
as the principle of *coherent integration from above*.
For example, in our investigation of some field in
nature we frequently come across a cluster of entities or
events which we cannot organise into coherent relation
with one another, but then find that they reveal an

intrinsic coherence when we consider them from a multi-levelled perspective. That is to say, the different entities or events that we are investigating begin to make rational sense when they are found to belong not to one and the same homogeneous level but to different while coordinated levels of connection. Usually this means that new factors, which we have failed to discern from the uniform perspective of the single level, are introduced into the picture from a higher level and bear upon the entities or events on a lower level in such a way as to assist their internal organisation into a coherent intelligible pattern. In this multi-dimensional perspective a profounder objectivity is disclosed.

All this applies not only to the stratification of each science but to the stratified structure which the various sciences manifest in their coordination with one another, for while each special science obeys its own disctinctive laws, each leaves undetermined certain boundary conditions which are open to control by operations of another science with a different set of laws on a higher level. Thus in nature itself the connections brought to light by physics and chemistry are found to be open to connections of a different kind obtaining in biological organisms, which for their part nevertheless rely upon the physico-chemical connections of their material components. Again, in our human interaction with nature we engage in engineering operations in which we impose designs and patterns upon nature in the construction of things like submarines or airships beyond what nature is capable of producing on its own. Yet all the time we rely on and do not infringe the laws of physics and chemistry, although we exercise some control over them through the boundary conditions where they are left undefined or open. Thus physico-chemical and biological relations in nature and physico-chemical and engineering operations in our technology harmonise in a stratification of orderly relations which gives them a richer and more meaningful coherence than they could have otherwise, but in accordance with the principle that each level of relations in the universe or in our scientific description of it is integrated through cross-level reference to the integration of a higher level. Thus we may claim that the universe is found to comprise interrelated levels of being, each of which is far from being closed in upon itself, but is open to and explicable in terms of its immediately higher level and indeed of the whole multi-levelled structure of the universe. As these different levels of reality become disclosed through our inquiries, together with the corresponding levels of our explanatory accounts of them, they combine with one another in such a hierarchical way as to constitute a vast semantic focus of meaning. While theoretically the number of these ascending levels might be conceived to be infinite, in the actual universe which is finite, the number is necessarily limited. So far as natural science is concerned, this must mean that the intelligibility or meaning of the whole semantic fabric demands and rests upon some ultimate self-sufficient ground of intelligibility as its sufficient reason, otherwise the whole of natural science would be finally pointless for its alleged intelligibility would run into nothing. Hence natural science through its remarkable intelligibility cries aloud for a proper doctrine of creation. So far as theological science is concerned, the created universe must be regarded as having been given and as sustained in its rational order, only in so far as it is open upward toward God the Maker of all things visible and invisible. That is to say, as a unitary intelligible whole the universe must be thought of as ultimately integrated from above through the creative bearing upon it of the Trinitarian relations in God himself.

BOOKS RELEVANT TO THIS CHAPTER

C. N. COCHRANE.

Christianity and Classical Culture. Revised edition. A Galaxy Book. Oxford University Press, New York, 1957.

A. EINSTEIN and L. INFELD,

The Evolution of Physics from early concepts to relativity and quanta. Simon and Schuster, New York, 1938.

A. EINSTEIN.

Ideas and Opinions. Souvenir Press, London, 1973.

M. POLANYI.

The Study of Man. Routledge and Kegan Paul, London, 1959.
The Tacit Dimension. Routledge and Kegan Paul, London, 1967.
Knowing and Being. Routledge and Kegan Paul, London, 1969.

W. BERKSON.

Fields of Force. The Development of a World View from Faraday to Einstein. Routledge and Kegan Paul, London, 1974.

HANS FREI.

The Identity of Jesus Christ. The Hermeneutical Bases of Dogmatic Theology. The Fortress Press, Philadelphia, 1967.

T. F. TORRANCE.

Space, Time and Incarnation. Oxford University Press, London, 1969.

Space, Time and Resurrection. The Handsel Press, Edinburgh, 1976.

The Ground and Grammar of Theology. University Press of Virginia, Charlottesville, and Christian Journals Limited, Belfast, 1980.

(Editor), *The Incarnation.* The Handsel Press, Edinburgh, 1980.

2.

The Priority of Belief

When the Royal Society of London was inaugurated in 1622 it adopted as its guiding motto the words *nullius in verba,* which might be translated 'on nobody's say-so', in acceptance of Francis Bacon's claim that natural philosophy must rely on purely empirical methods in repudiation of all external authorities. To understand the mysteries of nature we must put our questions directly to nature and follow only what it tells us about itself, without deferring at all to any arbitrary pronouncements and in distrust of all preconceptions and hypotheses. A year later, when the Royal Society was confirmed by the Crown, its charter given under the Great Seal, again echoing Francis Bacon, ruled that the investigations conducted by the fellows 'are to be applied to further promoting by the authority of experiments the sciences of natural things and of useful arts, to the Glory of the Creator, and the advantage of the human race'. Thus the charter which still governs the Royal Society makes it clear that the rejection of all external authority in the pursuit of natural science is not to be regarded as conflicting with belief in God, but on the contrary is to be regarded as a religious duty to the Creator.

This combination of the empirical stress on observations and experiments as the authoritative means of scientific knowledge with an overarching belief in God the Creator of the world and the Source of its rational order, was supremely exemplified in the position adopted by Isaac Newton. He held that 'natural philosophy consists in discovering the frame and operations of nature, and reducing them, as far as may be, to general rules or laws—establishing these rules by observations and experiments, and then deducing the causes and effects of things'. At the same time he held that the beautiful mechanical system of the world that becomes disclosed through such investigations could not have come from chance or any natural cause but could have come only from the counsel and contrivance of an intelligent all-powerful Being, the Maker and Lord of all things; and what is more, it could not continue to subsist without being conserved by his divine power and dominion. The universe is neither self-sufficient nor self-explanatory but as an orderly whole depends upon an intelligible and self-sufficient ground in the Creator who as the Supreme God exists 'necessarily'. Nevertheless the task of natural science is not to argue from any necessity in God or from any necessary connection between the universe and God, but to accept the universe as it came from the voluntary agency of God with the laws on which he chose to found it, and to determine those laws through inquiry into the causes that actually exist in the phenomena of nature.

Newton's way of coordinating belief in God the creative and sustaining Ground of all rational order in the universe and his explanatory account of the universal and uniform constitution of things by reasoning from mechanical principles alone, harbours a damaging ambiguity. He rejected any mechanical or necessary relation between the world and God the Creator, for that would have implied a God 'without dominion, providence and final causes who is nothing else but Fate and Nature'. Far from being the soul of the world — an idea which Newton abhorred — he is Lord over all, who governs and moves everything in the universe invisibly and freely through his will, the ever-living infinite, eternal, omnipresent, omniscient, omnipotent God. On the other hand, as we have seen, Newton worked with a concept of God as containing and ordering all things 'within his uniform sensorium', in such a way that neither God nor the world affects the other, for just as God suffers nothing from the motion of bodies so bodies find no resistance from the omni-presence of God. As such God constitutes a point of absolute rest or immobility by reference to which as a *vis inertiae,* or a force of inertia, all orderly phenomena in the universe may be plotted and described in terms of immutable natural law — the 'force of inertia' being defined by Newton as 'a form of inactivity'. This ambiguity between divine activity and passivity in Newton's thought is reflected in his account of the mechanical system of particles or bodies in motion of which the universe is made up, in terms of an 'active principle', such as gravity, which puts them in motion and of a 'passive principle', or inertial force, by which bodies persist in their motion or rest, but it is the latter which predominates in the geometric framework of his universal mechanics.

Deeply embedded in this outlook is a deistic relation between God and the creation which goes back not only to the medieval notion of the Unmoved Mover but to the thought of Francis Bacon who in a remarkable Confession of Faith published in 1611 identified 'the constant and everlasting laws which we call nature' with those actual laws which 'began to be in force when God rested from his work and ceased to create', i.e. laws in which God does not immediately and directly interact with nature. In Newton's outlook, however, this element of deistic inactivity is bound up with the interconnection of his theological and scientific concepts, for while his notion of the immutability and impassibility of God clearly influenced his conception of immutable natural law and universal mechanics, the latter through a powerful feed-back had a deep impact on his doctrine of God and his relation to the world. Moreover the massive synthesis of a deistic relation between God and the world and a hard epistemological dualism that took place when Newton distinguished between absolute and relative, true and apparent, mathematical and common, conceptions of time, space, place and motion and then clamped down absolute, true and mathematical time and space externally upon relative, apparent, common (or sensible) time and space, had the effect of building deism into the fabric of the new scientific culture and the kind of theology that arose within its constraints. It is that combination of deism and dualism that affected the whole history of modern theology down to our own day, and gave rise to the pseudo-problems from which theology is now being liberated, as we have seen, through fundamental change in the foundations of science.

Our immediate concern is with the steady effect of this combination of deism and dualism in driving a wedge between belief in God the Creator and the rational order of nature, and therefore between faith and reason. While Newton did not operate with an intrinsic relation between geometry and experience, or mathematics and nature, nevertheless through his profound faith in God as the creative Source of rational order he bracketed the theoretical and empirical poles of knowledge together in such a way as to give objective depth to his scientific account of the system of the world. That is to say, belief in God played a basic role in his thought prior to his scientific reasoning and continued to have a significant place in the ultimate premises of his natural science. The deistic element in that belief, however, which posited a relation of inertia or inactivity between God and the world, was bound to damage the bond between faith and reason and thereby also to undermine belief in an objective rational order independent of man. So far as the actual advance of human knowledge is concerned, God tended to be replaced by the fact of the rational order and harmony of nature, but when that lost its dimension of objectivity, the notion of God tended to fall away or to be relegated to man's inward private life.

That is precisely what began to happen in the empiricism of John Locke in Newton's own day, and in the positivist and conventionalist notions of science to which it gave rise. Locke worked with a radical dualism, corresponding to that of Galileo and Newton, between material substances, which obey purely mechanistic laws, and mental substances, which he conceived of as independent atomic entities or separated individuals. He reverted to the Aristotelian principle that there is nothing in the mind except what is first in the senses. Every one begins with a mind that is devoid of any innate or intuitive ideas and gains knowledge only through sense impressions received under the impact of material substances or through reflection on those impressions. This empiricist theory of knowledge led Locke to draw a sharp distinction between faith and reason or belief and rational knowledge. Belief is no more than an ungrounded persuasion or private opinion of the mind which falls short of knowledge, for it is not based on the evidence of the senses and is only extraneously related to what is believed. Rational knowledge, on the other hand, comes from experience and is established through demonstration operating with certain connections visible to our senses. This had the effect of reducing faith to a merely subjective state of affairs and of denigrating it as a cognitive act or a source of knowledge beyond the range of observation and demonstrative reasoning.

Locke's separation of faith and reason is also bound up with his extension of Newtonian deism, in a rejection of any dynamic interaction between God and the world which damaged and made even more ambiguous any connection between divine and human law. He certainly held that God is the Creator and Originator of the state of nature and of the law of nature which governs it, but that law of nature is now identified with 'the law of reason' — i.e. it is construed in accordance with the mechanistic conception of nature and its rational laws. Thus Locke's empiricism leads into an anthropocentric positivism in which priority is accorded to the 'law' of the autonomous human reason detached from and without reference back to an objective rational order independent of man. This line of thought was considerably reinforced when David Hume, operating with the same empiricist assumptions, called in question the objective character of causality or natural law by showing that the idea of necessary connections in nature upon which they depend cannot be derived from sensory experience but may be traced back to some form of 'natural belief'. From this it followed that the actual stuff of knowledge has to do only with the appearances of things to human subjects rather than with objects and their interconnections in the external world and with the way in which we associate or organise these appearances for our own convenience in life, without claiming that they bear upon ontological structures in any reality independent of our perceptions. The only thing we may be certain of or exact about is the relation of the ideas we derive in this way to one another, so that primacy must be given to logical clarity and consistency.

There is no need to pursue further the story of this phenomenalist and empiricist view of rational knowledge down the road it took through the Kantian synthetic *a priori* to the pragmatic conventionalism and anti-metaphysical nominalism of Ernst Mach in which it finally ran dry. However, several comments upon it must be made.

(1) With the rejection by Hume and Kant of belief in God from the fundamental convictions of rational knowledge, and certainly from the epistemological premises of natural science, the way was left open for a completely mechanistic conception of the universe and of human existence, including the enterprise of science in all its various forms, which left no room for belief or personal conviction. That led to the complete impersonalisation of science and human culture which we have already discussed in connection with Laplace. That is to say, the history of modern thought seems to teach us that a consistently empiricist approach to knowledge leads ineluctably to a self-contradictory outlook upon the universe in which the human person and conscious mind have no fundamental place.

(2) With a shift in the centre of gravity from a theocentric to an anthropocentric point of view, and an identification of natural law with the law of the autonomous reason, a rapid elimination of ontology and objectivity from the foundations of scientific knowledge sets in and there follows a serious lapse into scepticism. So long as belief in God even in a Newtonian way was bracketed together with the analytical and synthetical reduction of phenomena to rational order, science could be confident of gaining trustworthy knowledge of the universe, but if there is no controlling intelligible ground to which the apparent patterns of

nature are coordinated, how can they be accessible to rational analysis and scientific knowledge? If we are left to the uncertainties and limitations of our senses alone, without any reliance upon fundamental convictions which reach beyond sensation and observation, we can have no confidence in our ability to reach consistent and explicit rational knowledge.

(3) Further, with the disappearance of God from the scientific outlook upon the universe, the artificial dualist way of combining theoretical and empirical factors in knowledge, whether in a Newtonian or Kantian way, came to an end of its usefulness and became the source of serious error in the understanding and interpretation of nature. The phenomenal surface of experience began to disintegrate with the loss of its underlying coherence, so that highly abstract patterns of uniformity were imposed extrinsically upon it through the increasing rigour of analytical and instrumentalist methods, in the course of which science tended to be fused with technology to its own detriment in distortion of its meaning and purpose. Thus it steadily became clear that no profound advance in our knowledge of nature can be made if natural science inhibits itself from having anything to do with a reality beyond what is observable or from taking into rational account connections that are inherently unobservable. Science found itself face to face with the failure of the observationalist subject-object approach beyond limited levels of experience and inquiry, and was challenged by the need to penetrate behind sense-experience to the invisible object-object relations and dynamic field-structures which give continuity and cohesion to states of affairs in nature independent of our observations and manipulations. In other words, what was required was a profounder way of bringing theoretical and empirical factors together, in fact a

grasp of their inherence in one another both in nature and in our knowing of it. But how can that be gained if through the methods of observation we employ, the rational order of things in the universe is torn away from a frame of objective structures in reality or is made completely independent of an ultimate intelligible ground in God the Maker of all things visible and invisible?

That was the kind of problematic situation within which James Clerk Maxwell was at work in the third quarter of the nineteenth century, but with a mind deeply rooted in God. Like Michael Faraday, his older contemporary to whose vision of a new field-theory of the physical world he owed so much, he was a very devout person who believed, as he told the British Association in 1873, in the divine power and wisdom by which the worlds were created. This combination of profound faith in God and profound respect for the nature of the creation informed and prompted his scientific concern and made him unusually sensitive to the fundamental beliefs and epistemological grounds on which natural science must rest if it is to penetrate in any small measure into the mysteries of nature. That is to say, behind Clerk Maxwell's scientific outlook there lay an intuitive communication with God the infinite Author of all finite being, and with the whole cosmos from which man is physically and intelligibly inseparable, that constituted the unchangeable foundations of his confidence and at the same time gave him an awesome and humbling insight into the nature of created reality. The universe, as he understood it, is characterised throughout by a flexible structural relatedness — 'the divine process of nature' — in which man himself shares as a creature of God, in tune with which he is summoned to pursue his scientific inquiries. This is not to imply that Clerk Maxwell allowed the fundamental convictions he assimilated prior to his scientific reasoning to control that reasoning in any unwarranted way, for he constantly made a point of putting his controlling beliefs to the test in the course of his scientific inquiries and experiments by asking whether they yielded *tenable* theories and explanations, and by 'tenable' he meant whether they measured up in an acceptable way to the actual continuities and dynamic connections embedded in nature. Thus both the success and failure of scientific explanations served the critical clarification of his leading ideas, which far from weakening steadily strengthened his faith in the creative power and wisdom of God.

Several of these leading ideas must be noted for they played a crucial role in diverting the course of scientific thought away from the formalistic positivism in which empiricism had become trapped, and paved the way for the decisive alteration in our understanding of the universe that matured with Einstein.

(a)   Clerk Maxwell was convinced that the relations between things, whether so-called objects or events, belong to what things really are, for in nature all things are inseparably and ontologically connected together in the field in which they are found. In that case, relation is the most important thing to know, so that the determination of relations and the development of relational ways of thought must be allowed to have a primary place in scientific investigation and explan-ation. It is significant, however, that this idea of the relational character of the real world and of the need for relational thinking was not derived from his scientific reasoning but was brought to bear upon his scientific reasoning from a prior stock of theological and metaphysical convictions which had come to exercise a regulative role in his outlook upon the universe. It will be sufficient to recall that it was due to the development of relational thinking about the activity of God in creation and incarnation that enabled Christian theology to overcome the static container notion of space, and it was out of this relational thinking that there came the concept of the *person*, unknown in the world before Christianity, in accordance with which it was held that the relations between persons are of constitutive importance for they enter into what persons really are as persons. Thus an onto-relational way of understanding persons in community rejected an atomistic way of thinking of them as self-sufficient, independent, separated individuals who may be organised into a society only through their external relations with one another — the very notion into which John Locke disastrously carried European socio-political thought under the impact of Newtonian atomism and action at a distance. However, if it is in a relational way that we are to think of God's interaction with his creation and of our own creaturely inter-connections within it, why should a similar way of thinking not also govern our understanding of nature throughout the universe? From this perspective it need not surprise us to find that Clerk Maxwell's all-important 'break-through' came when he realised that his attempt to explain the electromagnetic field in accordance with the laws of Newton's mechanics was not finally 'workable', and produced an alternative account, *A Dynamical Theory of the Electromagnetic Field*, in which he made use of a relational, non-mechanical, way of thinking, while still employing the partial differential equations he had constructed for the non-viable mechanical model.

(b) Another of Clerk Maxwell's leading ideas, cognate to the one we have been discussing, is that 'nature abhors partition'. Classical science since Newton had thought of the universe as made up of

infinitesimal particles, and had developed analytical
methods of investigation through which things were
broken up into their component parts and then
considered in their external and mechanical connections with one another. Use was made of traditional
mathematics which operated in a similar way, by
dividing things up into an infinite number of mathematical points or units which are then considered in
their relations to one another and are manipulated in
sets of units or equations. This, said Clerk Maxwell,
had generally been supposed to be the most natural
method, but at best it could offer only 'partial explanations' of nature which are inevitably misleading for
they blind us to some of the most important facts.
Hence in the conviction that the idea of the *all* is
perhaps as primitive an idea as that of any individual
thing, he looked for another method in which we
proceed from the whole to the parts instead of from the
parts to the whole, and then seek to understand things
in their natural ensembles and continuities. It was this
conviction which predisposed him toward the concept
of field theory put forward by Faraday, but which
Clerk Maxwell developed in his own distinctive way
through his principles of relational or dynamical
reasoning. This is the concept of the continuous
indivisible field of relations characterised by inherent
dynamic structures which it is the task of science to
determine and express in the form of laws. So far as
contemporary science was concerned this had an
immense advantage over any theory based on observation alone which, because of the way our senses
operate in breaking up our apprehension of nature into
separated particulars, could only offer a discontinuous
account of nature. Its advantage was no less over the
purely analytical and mathematical formalism of
Laplace which, relying on Newton's notion of action at

a distance to explain the forces between particles of matter, gave rise to an extreme form of mechanical determinism which not only gave an unsatisfactory account of the actual process of nature but led to incorrect prediction—in any case, the notion of action at a distance was quite untenable. Einstein was later to claim that Clerk Maxwell's notion of field-theory was one of the greatest steps forward in the whole history of science.

(c)   The last of Clerk Maxwell's leading ideas we are to consider is that which he called 'embodied mathematics'. As we have seen he was dissatisfied with a purely analytical and formalistic mathematics, but that was out of concern for a more empirically relevant and appropriate mathematics which does not detach the processes of thought from contact with physical reality through the substitution of symbolic for real connections but allows the mind to lay hold of physical realities step by step through the development of 'physical conceptions'. He sought to steer a course between abstract theorising and pure experimentalism which would allow the actualities of nature to disclose themselves in fresh revelations to inquiry and inject new ideas into scientific understanding and reasoning. Looking back it would appear that Clerk Maxwell's aim to present mathematical ideas to the mind in an embodied form, and not as mere symbols which for all their logical certainty or consistency were not true to nature, was a move away from the Newtonian way of bracketing mathematics and nature or geometry and experience toward that which Einstein demanded and put into effect in relativity theory, one in which mathematical and empirical elements are intrinsically coordinated. Clerk Maxwell's embodied mathematics bears a very close relation to Einstein's conception of four-dimensional geometry indissolubly united to physics where it becomes a 'natural science' while providing physics with its internal epistemological structure. A distinct movement toward the unitary thinking of general relativity was certainly made through Clerk Maxwell's development of the notion of the continuous indivisible field in which field and matter were separate interpenetrating realities and his rejection of action at a distance which injected time into the material substance of the field, but Clerk Maxwell's attainment failed to realise its full potentiality for it retained an ultimate split between field and matter which was carried over from his attempts at a mechanical interpretation of the electromagnetic field along Newtonian lines. Nevertheless, the decisive step in the right direction had been taken, and Einstein was not slow to realise it as he thought out the implications of Clerk Maxwell's unification of light, electricity and magnetism in the dynamic field of radiation.

It was, I believe, Clerk Maxwell's profound faith in God the Creator that prompted him to set in motion this great change in scientific approach. Natural science was a way of looking at the universe and its marvellous patterns of order which fascinated and absorbed him, but he believed that it was God who made the universe like that and endowed it with its harmony and rational beauty, and so there must be another way of looking at the creation, from the perspective of the Creator. The explanations offered by natural science are inevitably partial and incomplete — the real explanations must lie beyond what the scientist can see with his eyes or work out with his mathematics. It was evidently this belief, together with his Christian theological way of understanding dynamic relations, which helped him to realise that a merely mechanical way of explaining how nature behaves was only partially valid — it was true up to a point but finally 'unworkable', as he said. However, all scientific theories are like that. God allows us to penetrate only so far into the mysteries of his creation and no more, for within finite and temporal existence there are limits beyond which natural science cannot go. For the scientist to regard the created universe in this way, *sub specie aeternitatis*, means that he must reckon with the fact that all his scientific knowledge is limited and provisional, and constantly needs to be revised until eternal Truth enlightens it.

Both James Clerk Maxwell and Isaac Newton were devout believers, but each thought of the relation of God to the creation in a different way. For Newton God provided, through the absolute time and space constituted by his eternity and omnipresence, the uniform unchangeable structure which ordered and underpinned the whole universe and to which Newton appealed as the fundamental framework for all scientific concepts and operations. In Newton's elaboration this was held to mean that God unceasingly bears upon the universe in an inertial way, causally conditioning all things within it and reducing them to a rigid mechanical system, but also that he exercises a regulative role within the system of efficient causal connections in order to prevent irregularities and conserve the harmony of the whole universe. It was that way of thinking that provoked the rejoinder of Laplace to Napoleon, *Je n'ai pas besoin de cet hypothèse,* for he claimed to be able to give such a complete account of the universe as a mechanical system according to self-regulating and eternal law alone that he had no need to appeal to any underpinning and adjusting activity on the part of Deity.

For Clerk Maxwell, on the other hand, God the living Creator could not be thought of as inertially related to the on-going universe in any deistic way which would give support to the notion of the universe as a closed necessary mechanistic system. He is the active and loving Father revealed through Jesus Christ his incarnate Son, who discloses to us the incomparable nature of his divine power and wisdom, and is creatively and invisibly at work in all the process of nature. He thought of God's relation to the universe as more transcendent and more intimate than that envisaged by Newton, but he did not introduce the concept of God as a formal factor into the conceptual structure of his scientific theories, far less as an intra-mundane Agent regulating the chain of efficient causes in connection with alleged irregularities in the solar and planetary system or with gaps in the scientific understanding of nature. Nevertheless, God was accorded a supreme place in Clerk Maxwell's ultimate beliefs which informed his scientific outlook and influenced his intuitive choice and formation of scientific ideas, so that he was constrained, along with Michael Faraday, to redirect the basic orientation of natural science in sharp divergence from the impersonal mechanistic outlook of Laplace and the continental determinist tradition.

The regulative role of fundamental belief and intuitive insight also characterised the scientific outlook and thought of Albert Einstein, to whom we now turn. More than any other he discerned the far-reaching implications of the new field-theoretical understanding of natural law and of the new mathesis it initiated in seeking to grasp the kind of form that actually inheres in the nature of what we try to apprehend. He rejected the Newtonian and Kantian approaches which in different ways removed certain fundamental concepts from the empirical domain to the intangible heights of an absolute or an *a priori* status where they were no more than empty conceptual schemata but where they were invested with a prescriptive and determinist role in our understanding of experience, and directed his attention to developing a new framework of thought grounded in the dynamic relatedness that permeates the actual universe. That is to say, Einstein objected to the separation resulting from classical dualism between 'the logical formal' and 'the objective or intuitive content' of mathematics, and switched his thought from abstract to embodied mathematics. He insisted on working with fundamental concepts of geometry that are associated with natural objects, for without that association geometry is neither true nor false and is worthless for the physicist. This was the all-important switch from Euclidean to four-dimensional geometry and the physical but dynamic space-time concepts it entailed, which meant working with ontologically grounded objectivities and intelligibilities that can never be completely reduced to conceptual explications or mathematical formalisations. In this event the scientist must learn to operate under the control of his ultimate beliefs and intuitive insights, but of course not without readiness to have them constantly put to the test in the course of his scientific reasoning which must always end with experience as well as begin with it. Far from implying any depreciation of the theoretical or mathematical components in physical knowledge this demand for intuitive contact with the real, which the abstract reason cannot touch, allows them to play a more basic and heuristic role in scientific activity. Einstein's own unparalleled achievements certainly justify his way of fusing together the logical-formal aspect and the intuitive content of mathematics.

Our immediate concern, however, is with the *priority* of fundamental belief in Einstein's conception and practice of scientific inquiry. In his essay on Clerk Maxwell's influence, he insisted, in sharp contrast to the positivist and conventionalist tradition, that 'The belief in an external world independent of the perceiving subject is the basis of all natural science', but along with that belief went another belief in the intrinsic comprehensibility of the universe. These are beliefs that have to be assumed and put to the test, but they are not open to logical derivation or proof for they are prior to logical reasoning and have to be employed as premises in any attempted proof. There could be no science without belief in the inner harmony of the world or without the belief that it is possible to grasp reality with our theoretical constructions. Belief of this kind, Einstein claimed, is and always will remain the fundamental motive for all scientific work.

In line with Clerk Maxwell, Einstein held that these fundamental beliefs are intuitive and religious in character. The intuitive character of belief is bound up with the mysterious and indeed miraculous fact which we can never understand that the universe is intelligible in itself and comprehensible to the human mind, but somehow there is 'a pre-established harmony' between human thought and independent empirical reality, in virtue of which the human mind can discern and grasp the relational structures embedded in nature. That is to say, it is only through *intuition, resting on sympathetic understanding of experience,* Einstein claimed, that we hope to arrive at the elementary laws which govern the cosmos.

It is worth noting that Einstein did not regard these regulative beliefs as 'primitive guesses' but as rational insights impressed on the mind by the objective lawfulness, harmony and beauty of the universe. The intuitive nature of these beliefs, together with the discovery of the marvellous beauty and simplicity of nature as they were disclosed, for example, through Clerk Maxwell's equations for the electromagnetic field or the equations of the general theory of relativity, evoked such profound awe from Einstein that he could not help but attribute to them a religious character. 'To the sphere of religion belongs the faith that the regulations valid for the world of existence are rational, that is comprehensible to reason. I cannot conceive of a genuine scientist without that profound faith. The situation may be expressed by an image: science without religion is lame, religion without science is blind.' It was in tune with this recognition of the religious character and overwhelming power of his intuitive beliefs that, when he was confronted with the rational order of things independent of us and absolute in the sense that we can have no control over it, Einstein instinctively spoke of it in theistic terms, as 'God' or, more familiarly, as 'the Old One'. Thus he would say 'God does not play dice' when insisting on a realist understanding of natural law, or 'God is sophisticated but not malicious' when referring to the reliability of nature, or would speak of some theory as 'closer to the secrets of the Old One', in so far as it penetrated into the inner truth and intelligibility of the universe.

How are we to interpret this? Was Einstein simply resolving God without remainder, so to speak, into the rational order immanent in nature? Some justification for this comes from a statement in which he equated 'a conviction of the rationality or intelligibility of the world lying behind all scientific work of a higher order' with 'firm belief in a superior mind that reveals itself in the world of experience', which he claimed to represent his conception of God. He associated this with Spinoza's 'pantheistic' notion of God. However, there is a problem about this, for in Spinoza's thought God and the universe constitute a necessary system which may be known through logico-deductive operations alone, but that is very far removed from the way Einstein understood the rational order of the universe. His difference from Spinoza's notion of God comes out in such a statement as 'God does not wear his heart on his sleeve' in which he points to a ground of rational order deeply hidden behind the appearance of things—that is to say, there is an element of the transcendent or the 'superpersonal', as he called it, in Einstein's belief in 'God' which is essential to his all-important idea of the invisible ultimate ground of reality and of the astonishing range of intelligibility disclosed in the universe which so far surpasses our powers of investigation that we may apprehend it only at relatively elementary levels. In this connection Einstein could write very movingly of 'that humble attitude of mind towards the grandeur of reason incarnate in existence, and which in its profoundest depths is inaccessible to man', or of 'rapturous amazement at the harmony of natural law, which reveals an intelligence of such superiority that, compared with it, all systematic thinking and acting of human beings is an utterly insignificant reflection'. In view of this it is perhaps not surprising that Karl Popper could refer to Einstein's thought as 'theistic'!

However, when Einstein likened his own view of God to that of Spinoza he seems to have had mainly in mind the latter's idea of God as impersonal infinite Being immanent in the universe, for it was precisely in the concept of a personal God providentially at work in the world that Einstein saw the main source of conflict between the spheres of religion and of science. That must surely be viewed against the background of the Newtonian association of God with the principle of inertia, namely, that something acts itself which cannot be acted upon. Einstein found this conception of inertia scientifically objectionable, but to cut that principle away from Newton's theology and science would have left him with the notion of a reciprocal relation between God and the universe in accordance with which God could be acted on : against which Einstein's Judaic intuition would have rebelled, and very rightly. Doubtless, from the perspective of another great Jewish thinker, Martin Buber, the question must be asked whether in the last analysis Einstein was not still constrained at this point by an impersonal model of thought. In any case it must be pointed out that the basic convictions prior to reasoning which gave insight and power to the Maxwellian reorientation of physics and which have borne such astonishing fruit in the achievements of the twentieth century, became effective through the steady abandonment of impersonal rationalistic models of thought. In this tradition Einstein has given immense support for the priority of fundamental belief as a compelling intuition of reality which it would be irresponsible and irrational to neglect or discount.

Before passing from Einstein's religious belief in the rationality of nature, let us listen to his own words.

'The most beautiful emotion we can experience is the mystical. It is the sower of all true art and science. He to whom this emotion is a stranger, who can no longer wonder and stand rapt in awe, is as good as dead. To know that what is impenetrable to us really exists, manifesting itself as the highest wisdom and the most radiant beauty, which all our faculties can comprehend only in their most primitive forms — this knowledge, this feeling, is the centre of true religiousness. In this sense and in this sense only, I belong to the ranks of devoutly religious men. The cosmic religious experience is the strongest and the noblest thing behind scientific research which is derived from it. No one who does not appreciate the terrible exertions, the devotion without which pioneer work in scientific thought cannot come into being, can judge the strength of the feeling out of which alone such work, turned away as it is from

immediate practical life, can grow. What deep faith in
the rationality of the structure of the world, what a
longing to understand even a small glimpse of the
reason revealed in the world, there must have been in
Kepler and Newton!'

No one has given more explicit discussion to the
priority of belief in rational knowledge than Michael
Polanyi who has contributed to the Maxwellian and
Einsteinian restructuring of the epistemological foundations of natural science with an unrivalled delicacy
and refinement. He made a particular point of re-
storing to rigorous scientific activity the personal
coefficient of knowledge and of showing that the
human reason never operates outside a framework of
basic beliefs. With Clerk Maxwell and Einstein he
rejected the positivist emphasis on abstract and
detached forms of thought which cut the reason off
from the very base in experience on which it operates,
and thus attacked the dualism between mind and
matter which leads to an unbalanced concentration
upon matter as though knowledge were restricted to
visible, tangible facts and their observable inter-
connections alone. But Polanyi went beyond Maxwell
and Einstein in showing that there can be no knowledge
even of material realities apart from the personal
activity of a knower and demanding that this personal
factor in scientific inquiry be brought out into the open
and be given its due place in the philosophy of science.
The emphasis upon an impersonal, detached approach
is meant to exclude from scientific knowledge all
subjective bias and prejudice, so that it can be
genuinely objective, but it must not be forgotten that
only a person is capable of self-criticism and of
distinguishing what he knows from his subjective states,
and therefore of appreciating the bearing of human

thought upon experience. In fact, it is only a person who can engage truly in objective and scientific operations. It must be recognised, therefore, that any scientific inquiry pursued in a detached, impersonal, formalistic way isolates itself from man's higher faculties and thereby restricts its range and power of insight and understanding. What science needs is a profounder approach in which it transcends the damaging split between subject and object or thought and experience, and recovers the natural unity of knowing and being, for without the integrative way of thinking that such a rational balance brings, science can only obstruct its own attempts to grasp the finer and more subtle patterns embedded in the continuities of empirical reality. That is to say, science needs to recover an appreciation of 'personal knowledge' in which the personal and the objective are fused together.

If the reduction of the epistemic relation between the human mind and reality to purely impersonal, formal-logical relations is destructive of the aims of science, as Einstein and Polanyi alike have demonstrated, then proper recognition must be given to the non-formal, or 'extra-logical' relation between the mind and reality, through which the mind acquires its fundamental intuitive content. That is to say, here we have to deal with the objective ontological reference of thought upon which all empirico-theoretical science depends, for without it knowledge could not even get off the ground. But it is precisely within this informal or extra-logical yet profoundly rational relationship that our basic beliefs emerge in the responsible commitment of the human mind to the compelling claims of intelligible reality upon it. This is why Michael Polanyi has insisted that we must recognise belief or intuitive apprehension once more as the source of knowledge from which our acts of discovery take their rise, for it is in belief that our minds are in direct touch with reality, in belief that our thought is open to the invisible realm of intelligibility independent of ourselves, and through belief that we entrust our reason to the rational order and reliability of the contingent universe. Behind and permeating all our scientific activity, whether in critical analysis or discovery, there is an elemental, overwhelming faith in the rational constitution of things, but faith also in the possibility of grasping the real world with our concepts, and above all faith in the truth over which we have no control but in the service of which our human rationality stands or falls. Faith and intrinsic rationality are interlocked with one another. No human intelligence, Polanyi claimed, however critical or original, can operate outside such a context of faith, for it is within that context that there arises within us, under compulsion from the reality of the world we experience, a regulative set of convictions or a framework of beliefs which prompts and guides our inquiries and controls our assessment of the evidence. They are the ultimate beliefs or normative insights grounded in reality on which we rely as premises in any authentic thrust toward truth, and which finally give our arguments any persuasive power they may have. Unless our minds are informed by prior intuitive contact with reality which we have in this way through our basic beliefs they flounder about in fruitless surmises and irrelevant interpretations and theories. Hence instead of shutting our eyes to these beliefs, we ought to bring them out into the open, put them to the test to distinguish them from subjective prejudices, and deliberately employ them in the actual process of scientific discovery and verification. It is after all under their regulative authority that we form our scientific judgements, make our decisions and carry through the reasoning operations of our inquiries to their true ends.

Several aspects of this position adopted by Michael Polanyi call for further elucidation.

(a) Polanyi's stress on the priority and controlling role of basic beliefs relates to his conception of 'the tacit coefficient in scientific theory', without which it has no bearing upon reality. While the formalisation of our knowledge in scientific theory deepens our grasp of reality and widens its range, it can never supercede but must continue to rely all through on informal acts of intelligence. In every dictionary the definition of any word relies on other undefined words to explain it, or to express it the other way round, a formal definition is the tacit reliance on certain undefined words to make clear the precise meaning of another word. It is not essentially different in the explicit, formal operations of science, for they rely at every stage in the process of inquiry upon implicitly or tacitly held beliefs that are grounded on the unalterable nature of things. That is to say, science does not operate from an axiomatic set of formally defined and verified propositions, as the positivists claim, but from ultimate informal assumptions which cannot be proved or refuted and which cannot be completely formalised, yet without implicit reliance upon them there would be no scientific knowledge at all. As examples of these ultimate assumptions we may refer to belief in truth or belief in the lawfulness of nature, neither of which we could prove for we would have to assume them in any attempted proof, but both of them are nevertheless all-determining constituents in our fundamental frame of belief, affecting the entire shape and scope of our scientific activities and their results as well. Hence Polanyi insisted that the premises of science on which all its inquiry rests are the beliefs held by scientists on the intelligible nature of reality independent of themselves and its capacity to disclose itself in an indeterminate range of yet unknown and perhaps yet unthinkable ways. Far from being subjective or irrational, these beliefs have to do with the structural kinship between the knowing subject and the objective reality he seeks to know, and they arise in his mind as intuitive convictions which he cannot reasonably avoid for they are thrust upon him as elemental aspects of reality pressing for realisation in his understanding.

(b) If all knowledge could be reduced to explicit formal relations, impersonal logical operations would take over completely and knowledge would be mechanised. However, those who hold such an absurd view — e.g. some advocates of so-called 'machine intelligence' or 'artificial intelligence'— fail to see that this is self-destructive, for the complete formalisation of all conceptual relations would sever them from the informal base on which they rest. In any case they forget that all the formal and symbolic equipment of scientific knowledge turns out in the end to be, like the computers we use, no more than effective sophisticated instruments for deploying our basic personal acts of knowledge and extending their range, and that it is powerless and useless unless it is held within a frame of personal insight and judgement. In all our fundamental acts of knowing we are engaged with the objective and ontological reference of our concepts to empirical reality, personal acts of participation by way of discernment, judgement, intention or decision in carrying out that reference, i.e. in relating ideas to experience, which are absolutely necessary. In other words, what Polanyi was concerned to do was to restore to its proper place in knowledge the responsible activity of the human person as a rational centre of consciousness. After all it is only a person who can think, mean, understand or interpret; only a person who can examine and weigh evidence in relating it to external reality, or who can appraise the validity of an argument; only a person who can discern a coherent pattern in nature and use it as a clue in the pursuit of his inquiry; only a person who can believe in truth and think and behave freely and yet as he must under obligation to it. All this does not mean that personal knowledge is subjective, for it is only a person who is capable of distinguishing objective states of affairs from his own subjective fantasies, and only a person who can engage in authentically objective operations. Personal knowledge, as Polanyi describes it, is a way of knowing through responsible commitment to the claims of reality in which the personal and objective poles of the relation are coordinated together in the act of establishing contact with reality and grasping it in its intrinsic rationality. As such, however, it cannot but have an essential place even in the most rigorous scientific operations, for without the tacit coefficient of the scientist's intuition and belief organising and integrating apprehension they would be fruitless and pointless. Michael Polanyi's rejection of the Laplacian impersonal model of thought and its replacement by another in which personal participation is shown to be essential to its rational and objective character, is a major contribution to the epistemological foundations of science.

(c) In line with this, Polanyi set out to clarify the fact that fundamental belief is objectively not subjectively grounded, in direct antithesis to Locke's discrediting of belief as no more than an ungrounded persuasion of the mind or a subjective feeling without evidential justification. Our fundamental beliefs are certainly personal convictions bound up with the elemental interaction between persons and realities other than themselves, but they are basic acts of acknowledgement in response to some intelligibility inherent in the nature of things, that is, to some meaningful order or message-laden pattern. As such they pivot upon the objective pole of the knowing relationship, and cannot be reduced to merely subjective states of consciousness. That is to say, beliefs arise in us because they are forced upon us by the nature of the reality with which we are in experiential contact, and as we allow our minds to fall under the constraint of its inherent intelligibility which we cannot rationally or in good conscience resist. Thus belief has to be understood strictly within the context of rational recognition of and willing sub-mission to the claims of objective reality upon us and of obligation towards the truth laid upon us by the truth itself. It is this ontological anchoring of belief in reality transcendent to ourselves which prevents it from being subjective or arbitrary, for it binds belief to what is independently and universally true. Properly speaking belief can be held only within the framework of a commitment to reality in which we assent to the universal validity of what we believe. Since belief and truth are correlated in this way, Polanyi points out that truth is the external pole of belief and belief, far from being a merely subjective or private concern, is to be regarded as the obedience of the mind to the truth in recognition of its universal claims and normative authority. However, while belief pivots upon the objective pole of the knowing relation, the subjective pole must be given its proper if subordinate place, i.e. the role of the person or rational agent in believing, and believing as he is convinced he ought to believe in fidelity to the truth. As Polanyi expresses it: 'The freedom of the subjective person to do as he pleases is overruled by the freedom of the responsible person to act as he must'. That is what is so distinctive about scientific belief, the combination of personal and compulsive elements in it. Polanyi brings these two elements together in his notion of commitment in which freedom and obligation, conscience and obedience, are bound inseparably together under the overarching authority of truth.

In concluding this discussion on the priority of belief two comments may be offered.

In the first place, the reorientation that has been taking place in the foundations of scientific knowledge, which we have traced from Clerk Maxwell through Einstein to Polanyi, demands that we must recognise belief or intuitive apprehension once more as the source of knowledge from which our acts of discovery take their rise, for it is in belief that we are in direct contact with reality and through belief that our minds remain open to the invisible realm of intelligibility independent of ourselves and whatever it may yet disclose to us of itself. Regarded in this way, faith and rationality are intrinsically bound together. It must be granted, as we have noted, that by their nature beliefs of this kind are not themselves directly or logically demonstrable, for they have what Einstein called 'extra-logical' status, but they are nonetheless rational. They are concerned not with the relations of ideas or indeed with relations of matters of fact, but with the relations of ideas to being which cannot be put into logical or rationalistic form. They are logically prior to any demonstration for they have to do with the bearing of reason on the nature and structure of things, which all explicit forms of reasoning are intended to serve and without which they are blind and impotent. In this event it is un-reasonable to throw faith and reason into a Lockean 'contradistinction', for faith is the very mode of rationality which the reason takes in its faithful adapt-ation to what it seeks to understand and explain. That is to say, here we recover the epistemic process in which, as historic Christian theology has so often claimed, we believe in order that we may understand, while in the course of developing our understanding we test and clarify our beliefs and thereby strengthen the hold of authentic belief upon our minds. There is, then, a formal similarity in the functioning of scientific belief and theological belief, but a proper difference between them must be taken into account. If belief or faith is correlated with the intrinsic rationality of the object and its self-evidencing reality and revealing power, that applies in different ways in accordance with the specific nature of the reality concerned. It is to be accepted, therefore, that belief in God calls for a mode of response in accordance with his nature as the transcendent Ground of all created being and intelligibility, but for that reason faith involves an intensely rational and not a blind commitment to God, in the course of which there ought to take place a steady sifting out of true from false belief.

In the second place, the transition that has been taking place away from abstract, formalistic and impersonal modes of thought to one in which the personal coefficient of knowledge is restored in the proper balance of our cognitive powers, demands that we recognise the personal character of fundamental belief. However, that must also be understood differently in natural scientific and in theological inquiry. In natural science in which we interact with realities which are not themselves centres of rational consciousness, except in so far as human beings are included among them, the personal coefficient must function rather differently. In theological inquiry, however, we are concerned with God himself who is not only the transcendent Creator of all contingent reality but the creative Source of all personal being in the universe, and who reveals himself to mankind through the acute personalisation of all his relations with them in the

incarnation of his eternal truth and love in Jesus Christ.
Here, then, we have to reckon with a personal factor on
both sides of the knowing relationship: we know God
only through intelligible communion with him. This
means that the personal character of belief in the
knowledge of God is much more intense than in our
knowledge of the physical world. In one sense it is also
much more objective, for the objective pole of knowledge is the Lord God who by his very nature objects to
the imposition of our subjective notions on him, not to
speak of any misguided attempts to bring him within
the range of our controlling knowledge. Now in
theological inquiry we are unable to hold apart this
intensely personal understanding of God from our
understanding of him as the ultimate intelligible
Ground of the universe. From the perspective of
theology, therefore, the ultimate intelligible Ground of
the universe, which is the sufficient reason for the
intelligible states of affairs in the universe disclosed by
natural science, is personal. Indeed he is the one self-
sufficient Person who is the Source of all personal being
other than himself. How are we to think of this from
the perspective of natural science, which has also to
face the question as to the ultimate intelligible Ground
of the universe and its contingent rational order? That
question is even more pressing, now that science has
had to introduce the concept of time into its explanations of the dynamic, contingent states of matter in a
finite universe, for it can no longer escape the question
as to the origin and end and therefore the 'why' of the
universe, if it is to retain belief in the objective reality
and unitary intelligibility of the universe. This is not to
imply that natural science can answer the question
which in some form it is bound to raise, but if it
recognises that the universe through its intelligibility
points beyond itself to an ultimate self-sufficient

Ground, and reckons with Polanyi's reintroduction of the personal model of thought into its epistemological foundations, it must surely go beyond the impersonal conception of Einstein, in entertaining the conception of a personal God as the creative Source of all the meaning and rational order disclosed through its investigations of nature. At any rate, Michael Polanyi has argued, from within the perspective of natural science, not only that emancipation from an impersonal conception of knowledge opens up a meaningful world which can resound to religion, but also that the multi-levelled structure of reality brought to light through inquiry sweeps thought on through the notion of an ascending hierarchy of meaning to envisage the meaning of the universe as a whole, in which 'natural knowledge continuously expands into knowledge of the supernatural'.

BOOKS RELEVANT TO THIS CHAPTER

E. A. BURTT.
The Metaphysical Foundations of Science. Revised edition. Doubleday Anchor Books, Garden City, N.Y., 1932.

H. S. THAYER.
Newton's Philosophy of Nature. Selections from his Writings. Hafner, New York and London, 1953.

A. EINSTEIN.
The World as I See It. John Lane, London. 1935.
The Meaning of Relativity. Fifth edition. Princeton University Press, Princeton, 1956.

P. A. SCHILPP (editor).
Albert Einstein: Philosopher-Scientist. Tudor, New York, 1957.

L. INFELD.
Albert Einstein. His Work and Influence On Our World. Charles
Scribner's Sons, New York, 1950.

J. BERNSTEIN.
Einstein. Fontana/Collins, London, 1953.

J. AGASSI.
*The Continuing Revolution: A History of Physics from the Greeks
to Einstein.* McGraw-Hill, New York, 1968.

W. D. NIVEN (editor).
The Scientific Papers of James Clerk Maxwell. Two Volumes.
Cambridge University Press, Cambridge, 1890.

RICHARD OLSON.
Scottish Philosophy and British Physics 1750-1880. Princeton
University Press, Princeton, 1975.

MICHAEL POLANYI.
Personal Knowledge. Routledge and Kegan Paul, London, 1958.
Science, Faith and Society. With new introduction. Chicago
University Press, Chicago, 1964.
F. Schwarz (editor), *Scientific Thought and Social Reality: Essays
by Michael Polanyi.* Psychological Issues, Vol. viii/Number 4,
Monograph 32. International Universities Press, New York, 1974.

T. F. TORRANCE
Karl Barth. Introduction to His Early Theology 1910-1931.
S.C.M., London, 1962.
'The Place of Michael Polanyi in the Modern Philosophy of
Science'. *Ethics in Science and Medicine.* Volume 7, Number 1,
pp. 57-95. Pergamon Press, Oxford, 1980.
(Editor), *Belief in Science and in Christian Life: The Relevance
of Michael Polanyi's Thought for Christian Faith and Life.* The
Handsel Press, Edinburgh, 1980.

3.

The Theology of Light

In the course of scientific investigations into the contingent universe new ideas introduced by Clerk Maxwell and Einstein, enabling us to penetrate more deeply into the subtle harmonies and symmetries of nature, have forced us to recast our understanding of the physical structure of the universe. At the same time we have also had to recast the cognitive structure of the scientific enterprise itself, for, as we have seen, through the interaction of the inquiring mind and the intelligibilities of objective reality there becomes disclosed a structural kinship between human knowing and what is known. Nothing has occupied a more significant place in these developments than the deepening conception of *light*. This is very evident in the switch from a mechanistic to a relational interpretation of nature and in the corresponding change in our understanding of natural law as expressing the dynamic structure of the continuous field, but it is also manifest in the central and unifying role of light across the whole spectrum of scientific knowledge.

James Clerk Maxwell's discovery of the mathematical properties of radiation enabled him to develop equations which could bring all the phenomena of luminous and electromagnetic radiation together in a single theory, and in so doing he unified optics and electromagnetism in a remarkable synthesis. It took some time for the implications of these revolutionary developments to be grasped, but it became clear to science that light represents the most fundamental form of radiation in the electromagnetic field and behaves in a way that defies mechanical explanation. Then after the work of Hertz and Lorentz on the consequences of Maxwell's theory, Einstein drew the threads together in an even wider synthesis in which he unified mechanics and Maxwell's theory through his development of the special and the general theories of relativity. Moreover, in his early contribution to quantum theory he introduced the conception of *photons,* demanding the quantisation of the electromagnetic field, which led to the recognition that light and matter are not only interrelated but ultimately only different manifestations of energy. Light turns out to be the most refined form of matter. Thus in virtue of its nature light has a supreme place among physical realities in the universe and in virtue of its unparalleled speed a unique role in linking and coordinating them all together within its rational harmony. In this way through the discovery of light, by reference to which the whole space-time framework of empirical reality is to be understood, modern physics has brought us to the conception of the universe as *a universe of light.* It is in the light of light itself that our minds have been able to reach this conception. Hence, as de Broglie pointed out, light has rendered us the fundamental service not only of illuminating the nature of physical existence but of enlightening our minds at the same time.

Such is the marvellous universe of space and time which God has created and to which we belong as those creaturely constituents through whose exploration and description the universe unfolds its rational harmony and beauty. It is structured and ordered throughout in accordance with the principle of the primacy of light which God has given it from its very beginning. The immense extent of the universe, judged by the time it takes rays of light to traverse it at the fantastic speed of about 186,000 miles per second, is utterly overwhelming. Judged by the same standard, the finite speed of light, the universe is finite, yet since it is found to be continuously expanding at a rate approaching the speed of light, it is also unbounded in a double sense: it extends its boundaries and breaks through the bounds of our comprehension. Nevertheless, it reveals itself throughout to be constituted and flooded by light, which in spite of its vast difference is surely a created reflection of the uncreated and unlimited Light which God himself is.

Since it is through his self-revelation to us in the universe that we realise that God has established a relation of dependence and created correspondence between its contingent rationality and his own transcendent rationality, we may be allowed to use our understanding of physical or created light as a foil for articulating our understanding of divine or uncreated Light. This is not to say that the Light of God may be understood only as it depends on and is conditioned by created light as a necessary medium and carrier for its movement. One of the remarkable consequences of Clerk Maxwell's theory, not discerned by him but uncovered by Einstein, is that physical light itself has no need of a medium such as 'ether' to support its transmission. How much less does the creative Light of God, which is the source of all light and all intelligible media in the universe, need any means of transmission other than its own force to reach us! While we are concerned here to articulate a theology of light within the context of a scientific culture permeated by a deepening understanding of physical light, we must bear in mind that, owing to the vast unlikeness between created and uncreated light, any analogies drawn from the former are to be regarded as more helpful to ourselves than as appropriate to the latter. Analogies, comparisons or illustrations taken from created realities are properly employed, not to bring our understanding of the Creator within the measure of our creaturely conceptions, but rather to aid the expression and communication of what we apprehend apart from them. On the other hand, the point must be made that, far from discounting or depreciating created light, uncreated Light constitutes the ultimate ground of its intelligibility and as such establishes it and gives it its true value. Apart from such a basis in uncreated Light all our experience and knowledge of things in the universe would finally be meaningless, for they would be devoid of any ultimate standards of truth, goodness or beauty.

(1) Let us begin with the *constancy* of light, or rather with the fact that light is always propagated in empty space with a definite, unsurpassable and constant velocity. It was by assuming this principle, together with the principle of relativity for all uniform motions, that Einstein developed his theory which has altered our whole picture of the physical universe. It is important to realise that the constancy of the speed of light in all systems is not a derivative but an ultimate principle with an independence of its own. While all entities and events in the universe are defined relationally in terms of space and time, and space and time are defined relationally in terms of light, light is not defined by reference to any contingent reality beyond itself. In other words, 'light has a unique metaphysical status in the universe'. That was the point discovered by Einstein when he established that the speed of light remains the same irrespective of any motion in its source or of any motion on the part of the observer. A

helpful analogy might be taken from the way in which
the configurations of waves set in motion by the
movement of a ship remain the same independent of
the movement of the ship or of any observer — although
that of course does not explain the behaviour of light.
All things naturally appear different to different
observers, for they are relative to their perceptions and
their positions in space and time, but the staggering
fact about light is that the constancy of its speed
remains the same for all observers through all those
relativities, no matter where they are or how fast or
slow they may move. No one can be in a privileged
position, for the speed of light in different systems of
time and place, of which one is in motion relative to
another, remains constant. Since this implies that one
observer's time is different from another observer's
time — really and not just apparently different, for
space and time cannot be separated from one another
but constitute a continuous indivisible field — it became
clear to Einstein that the notions of absolute space and
time of classical physics, which constituted a homogeneous unchanging system, had to be dismantled and that
the concepts of space and time had to be rethought very
radically as relative features of actual on-going events
contingent upon the propagation of light. This is
precisely what he did in developing relativity theory.
The constancy of the speed of light thus turns out to be
an utterly invariant feature of the universe, which
means that on the actual plane of reality all descriptions of orderly events in nature, i.e. all natural laws,
must have the same form and value for all observers,
quite contrary to apearances or common sense notions
such as the relativity of velocities. We find it strange
that while the speed of a bullet in the air fired from a
moving car is the speed of its propulsion from the gun
plus the speed of the car, the speed of a light signal sent
from the same car remains constant.

We may express the same point in another way by saying that, through the constancy of its immense unsurpassable speed and its supremacy over all space and time, light behaves in the same equable way toward all that takes place within the universe, and as such provides an invariant and reliable, while dynamic, base, for all its regularity and order. It should be appreciated that invariance is a realist and not a determinist concept. It has nothing to do with the rigid necessity that characterised the static structure of causal connections imposed on our understanding of nature by the framework of absolute isotropic time and space. Rather does invariance refer to a dynamic relatedness inherent in the empirical universe which through the space-time metrical field gives objective, reliable configuration to all our experiences within it. Thus the unique and central role of the speed of light and its uniform constancy enable modern science to interpret and explain the phenomena of nature with a profounder and more unrestricted notion of objectivity than was possible for classical physics. Of course, if the behaviour of light were not constant but arbitrary and variable, nothing would be certain, for the universe would be characterised by utterly random fluctuations and sheer irregularity. That is to say, what we regard as the universe would constitute chaos, not a cosmos, and certainly no objective or rational knowledge could emerge within it. The universe is profoundly intricate and mysterious and full of surprises, but far from being arbitrary it manifests everywhere throughout all change and fluctuation an integrity and trustworthiness which are to be associated with the invariant properties of light.

No doubt the question must be asked how the universe in the first place came to have this all-significant relation to light and how light itself came to have these properties which make for the emergence and continuity of its order and harmony. This is a question about the initial, given conditions of the universe which, if the universe is the intelligible system it is, could not have been simply chaos. How could a status of chaos in the first instance act with sufficient regularity and lawfulness to give rise to the general laws of motion in terms of which the order and beauty of the cosmos are to be explained? It was through reflection on that question in his early work on *Cosmogony* that Immanuel Kant found that rational understanding of the universe has to reckon with the existence of God, at least in setting it all going, or as we might say programming into it its initial conditions in the fundamental properties of light. That is to say, the universe would have no ultimately reliable base for its rational order, if the primacy and constancy of physical light were not ultimately grounded in the self-sufficient uncreated Light of eternal God. Only chaos can come out of chaos, but constancy can come only from an ultimate source of Constancy unconditioned by anything other than itself.

Our interest here, however, is not with the so-called 'cosmological argument', but with the actual reliability and trustworthiness of the universe, the orderly state of affairs which we now learn to interpret through reference to the constancy of light, for it does help us, I believe, to appreciate in a new way the constancy or faithfulness of God. After all, this astonishing universe is none other than the universe which God has created and unceasingly sustains in relation to his unlimited rationality and inexhaustible source of possibility. In endowing it with its marvellous order God has given it a covenanted correspondence to his own Mind and Will as Creator, within which he has made himself known and manifested his faithfulness to all that he has made.

The created light immanent in the universe does not of itself enable us to know the uncreated Light of God, far less to gain access into his Mind and Will, but it does help us to express the knowledge of his faithfulness as Creator and Preserver mediated to us through God's self-revelation and self-communication to mankind, which he has brought to its fulfilment and anchored in our space-time existence in Jesus Christ. All that we know of Jesus Christ 'the same yesterday, today and for ever' justifies us in believing in God's unchanging and unconditional faithfulness. As the uncreated Light of God incarnate, he constitutes the ultimate pledge given to us by God of the unfaltering consistency and the steadfastness of his love toward us. Thus it is by reference to Jesus Christ as *the Light of the World,* i.e. as the divine *Constant* in space and time, that we may interpret the orderly ways and works of God within the cosmos, but it is also through the way that those ways and works within the cosmos reflect back upon God that aspects of his Constancy may be focussed in sharper definition for us.

A fundamental aspect of God's Constancy is his *Truth.* In the Biblical revelation the faithfulness, reliability and truth of God are cognate conceptions, for they all have to relate to the fact that in being who he uniquely, eternally and invariably is, God is the one Constant upon whom all the coherent orderliness and harmony of things visible and invisible, tangible and intangible, finally depend. That is to say, God is the exclusive Ground and Source of all absolute standards, and thereby rejects the absolutising of any other standards in heaven or earth. This is surely the significance of the preface to the Ten Commandments: 'I am the Lord your God . . . You shall have no other gods before me'. Another way of expressing this would be to say that in constituting the ultimate objective

Basis of all truth God confers relativity upon the realm of all our human conceptions and statements about him.

This is an aspect of the invariant truth and reality of God that we may throw into relief through what we understand of the behaviour of physical light in the universe. On the one hand, the fact that light invariably takes the shortest path or the least time in travelling between two points requires us to reject the consideration of any other possibility. Thus natural law which is finally governed by the unique, unsurpassable and constant behaviour of light must take on an exclusive form. On the other hand, as the theory of relativity makes clear, the grounding of objectivity upon an invariant relatedness inherent in nature, has the effect of conferring relativity upon all our perceptions and conceptions of it. We operate, therefore, with a twofold invariance, a mathematical and an ontological. Under the rational pressure of nature itself upon our minds we construct a mathematical form of invariance as a model with which to offer a theoretical account of the objective invariance immanent in the universe, but in so far as that objective or ontological invariance becomes disclosed through the mathematical model, it discriminates itself from it and relativises it. However, in so far as the ontological invariance thus revealed points beyond itself to an ultimate independent ground of invariance which confers consistency upon its intelligibility, it is itself thereby relativised as having only a contingent and not an independent or necessary status in the universe. In other words, the light-related invariance in the universe is neither self-sufficient nor self-explaining : its ultimate truth lies beyond itself in the utterly constant and invariant nature of God's eternal Being.

It is because God himself is so absolutely faithful that

the universe described by reference to the constancy of physical light is so invariantly reliable. God does not play dice, as Einstein used to say. Conversely, through its bearing upon the contingency and relativity of all invariance immanent in the universe God's own eternal faithfulness presses for deeper realisation and appreciation in our minds. It must not be forgotten, however, that as the supreme Light, the Source of all light, God is the Creator not only of sun and moon and stars and all light in the universe, but also of the light of the human mind, so that the relativisation of the whole created order applies to all human conceptions and formulations, theological as well as scientific. On the other hand, because the uncreated Light of God remains utterly constant and faithful, irrespective of the vagaries of our human actions and conceptions, we are called to serve the invariant dynamic rule of his holy Love in the history of the creation and to commit our minds freely to the universal claims of his immutable Truth as the ultimate standard for all our conceptions and formulations in human inquiry.

Another aspect of God's Constancy which we may consider is his *Grace*. God is wholly and unconditionally gracious. Grace may be described as the consistently free and unreserved self-giving of God in love to all alike, which is not conditioned or controlled in any way whatsoever by the worth of its object. It is the constant and ceaseless out-flow of the Love of God which has no other reason for its movement than the Love that God is, and is therefore entirely without respect of persons and irrespective of their reactions. In the Biblical tradition this conception of the undeserved Grace of God is allied to an understanding of a covenant relationship of steadfast love and truth between God and his people. While covenant relationship was disclosed through its concrete realisation in God's

relations with historic Israel, it has been unilaterally set
up by God between himself and all mankind, to which
he remains everlastingly faithful and which he unilaterally upholds no matter whether the covenant
partner fulfils his part in the relationship or not. God
can no more break his covenant of Love and Truth
with mankind than he can cease to be God. The unilateral character of his covenant relationship and the
unconditional nature of Grace on which it rests have
steadily met with resistance in ancient and modern
times on the part of men and women. Through deeply
ingrained habits (that is, by virtue of our original sin)
we want in some measure to deserve or earn the Grace
of God — hence even the prodigal cannot repent
without asking his father to take him on as one of his
'hired servants'. Thus we tend regularly to interpret
God's unilateral covenant mercies within a frame of
thought, such as the so-called 'covenant of works'
invented by Calvinists, in which the self-giving of God
in undiluted Grace is held after all to be conditional on
our human responses. However, it was precisely in
order to save us from that state of affairs, in which we
are thrown back on ourselves where we are trapped in
our own self-regard and self-will, that Jesus came
preaching the Gospel of the sovereign unconditional
Grace of God which is poured out freely on all people
alike whether they are reckoned to deserve it or not.
Indeed, if any discrimination is to be made it is made
in favour not of the righteous but of sinners, not of the
healthy but of the sick. This radical objectivity of God's
Grace was stressed by Jesus when, for example, in his
Sermon on the Mount he taught that God 'makes his
sun to shine on the evil and the good, and sends rain on
the just and the unjust'. That is to say, out of his sheer
unmerited Grace God makes his uncreated Light to
shine in the same free, invariant and equable way on

all that he has made, for such complete impartiality on the part of God's Grace has the effect of relativising all our interpretations of it.

We may underscore this Biblical emphasis on the thoroughly consistent and impartial operation of God's Grace in the creation, through referring back again to the special theory of relativity which is based, as we have seen, on the constancy of light in all empirical systems. This revealed the exalted and unchanging character of light as it behaves throughout the universe in an objectively equal and 'impartial' way, for it is not caught in or conditioned by any of the physical structures or systems dependent on it, but remains supreme above them all. *Mutatis omnibus mutandis,* it may be said that the transcendent and invariant operation of divine Grace bears upon human life and history in such a way that it is not entangled in or tied to or conditioned by the spatio-temporal relations, empirical structures or inter-personal reciprocities in our creaturely existence, but remains supreme above them all. Strange and astonishing as we may find it, God makes all things operate together for good, regardless of the divergencies of human reactions to his saving Love, because his Grace is so sovereignly free and unlimited in its possibilities that in his interaction with humanity God provides the invariant but dynamically objective Ground for the fulfilment of his eternal purpose in the creation. Thus far from being antinomian, the unconditional Grace of God acts in such a creative and redemptive way upon human life and history that it makes them, and indeed all that takes place within the creation, serve the invariant laws of God's eternal Love.

At no point perhaps is it more requisite for those of us who come from the Augustinian and Calvinist traditions to understand the utter consistency and

faithfulness of God than in the doctrine of predestination or election. We shall return to consider this
doctrine in the succeeding chapter, but at the moment
it will be sufficient to stress the fact that God's Grace is
invariably equal and impartial toward the obedient
and the disobedient, the believing and unbelieving,
alike. If people are ultimately damned, that cannot be
due to some 'No' in the judgement of God against them
in contrast to a 'Yes' in favour of others, for as St. Paul
insisted there is no duality of 'Yes' and 'No' in God but
only the 'Yes' of his Grace. The Grace of God is
invariantly the same — nothing can overtake it or
deflect it — but precisely because of its invariance it is
exclusive of those who, for some ununderstandable
reason, want to isolate themselves from the Love of
God. In the unrelenting invariance of his Grace to all
alike God remains for ever consistently true and faithful
to the Love that he is as God.

(2) We turn from considering the constancy of light
to consider its *invisibility*. What help may we derive
from this paradoxical property of light in drawing out
the theological implications of the invisibility of God
and making them understandable in our universe of
created light? The realisation that we cannot see light
itself but only things lit up by light and of the relevance
of this fact for our knowledge of God has a long history
in Judaeo-Christian thought. God is himself the
supreme Light, unapproachable and invisible, but he
is illuminatingly present in the world of thought as the
created light of the sun is in the world of sense — yet
somehow the nature of created light reflects the
invisibility of God as well as his power of illumination,
since in a strange way physical light is at once a
darkness in itself and yet the source of brightness all
round it. It was as such that light was the first of all
created realities to be called by God into existence that

from the very beginning it might irradiate the heavens and the earth. All this implied a fundamental principle (which classical Greek thought had developed in another form) namely, that the invisible is not to be explained in terms of the visible but the visible is to be explained in terms of the invisible.

In the early centuries of the Christian era there emerged a fascinating Patristic theology of light which has left its mark upon the whole history of Christian thought. This took shape largely through a struggle between the teaching of the Biblical revelation and Mandean and Hellenic ideas, and gave rise to a clear-cut distinction between uncreated and created light in opposition to the pagan dichotomy of reality which placed all intelligibility in the world within the realm of the divine. In the West it is St. Augustine who stands out as the great theologian of light, in whose writings all the features of light mentioned above are developed in their symbolic signification. He operated with a three-fold distinction between the physical light of nature, the intelligible light of the mind, both of which are created, and the uncreated intelligible Light of God. However, this distinction was cast within a general epistemological framework of a dualism between the intelligible and the sensible realms, which tended to trap Augustine's thought in an ambiguous compromise with Platonic theory, in accordance with which he held that the created light of the human intellect is capable of knowledge only in so far as it participates in the eternal uncreated Light of God — an idea often referred to as 'ontologism'.

In the East the outstanding thinker concerned with light was John Philoponos of Alexandria. Working from a solid base in the teaching of Athanasius, Basil, and Cyril of Alexandria, he drew out the implications of the theological distinction between uncreated and

created reality for the understanding of the contingent
nature of the universe and its unitary rational order,
thereby undermining and discarding the epistemological dualisms of Neoplatonists and Aristotelians
alike. Through commitment to Christian belief in 'God
the Father Almighty, Maker of heaven and earth and
of all things visible and invisible', he rejected any
cosmological dichotomy between heaven and earth for,
since celestial as well as terrestrial matter belong
together within the same domain of creation, there is
no essential difference under God between them. He
also repudiated entirely any notion of the eternity of
the world on the ground that the invisible geometrical
forms of its rational order in space and time came into
being in and with the creation of the universe out of
nothing, and thus in the last analysis are no less
contingent in their rational nature than material
reality. In this understanding of God's creation the
distinction between created and uncreated light played
an essential part, for it led Philoponos to develop a
remarkably advanced physics of light in which he
translated into empirical terms both the relational
conceptions of space and time developed by the theologians and the notion of impetus or motion implied in
the doctrine of creation. From the radiant activity of
God's supreme Light which streamed into the creation,
created light was diffused throughout the universe
imparting to it all its energy. According to Philoponos
this physical light is not only the most rarefied form of
matter but itself a source of activity or energy in the
form of rays which travel in straight lines at an infinite,
invisible speed and which do not behave in mechanical
ways. Thus the whole of the contingent universe is to be
regarded as pervaded and configured by the kinetic
behaviour of light, under the creative and sustaining
power of God's uncreated Light. It is significant that

this physics of light elaborated from basic theological convictions had the retroactive effect of clarifying and reinforcing Philoponos' understanding of the relation of God to the universe, which allowed him to make effective use of analogies taken from the properties of physical light in seeking to elucidate the operation of uncreated divine Light in the incarnation of God's eternal Word in Jesus Christ, 'by whom all things were made'.

Some of these scientific conceptions deriving from John Philoponos and mediated to the West through Simplicius and Alghazali, came together with the theology and metaphysics of light which emanated from St. Augustine. This is nowhere more evident than in the *cosmogony of light* developed by Robert Grosseteste in the thirteenth century in accordance with the claim that optics is the primary physical science. He argued that physical light, which is the original and fundamental substance of God's creation, extends itself unceasingly throughout the universe in such a way as to constitute the form of corporeal reality and to be the underlying cause of all change and motion. Here too, then, a conception of the creation as a universe of light is held under the overarching principle that the eternal Light of God is the Light of all things by which their light is lighted.

We cannot enter further into the history of these ideas but sufficient has been said to indicate something of the conceptual outlook which resulted from a continuing interaction between theological and scientific understanding of the nature and function of light, for it enabled theologians to make more understandable the Biblical teaching that while God himself dwells invisibly in 'unapproachable Light' he is nevertheless the Source of all illumination in the universe. Scientific ideas about this universe in which God has set mankind have changed and developed throughout the centuries, but there has persisted the conviction that the true natures of things become more evident to us as they are lit up by a light which is in itself strangely invisible. Through the mystery of the invisibility of light God guards and reflects the mystery of his own invisible Light before which our creaturely finite minds falter and fail, but nevertheless he allows us, as St. Paul expressed it, to 'see' him darkly or indirectly as in a mirror.

Let us take our cue at this point from St. John of the Cross in the aftermath of the Reformation, for whom these enigmatic words of St. Paul had a special significance. Steeped in the historic theology of light he was absorbed by the discovery that the most intimate and illuminating knowledge of God comes through experiencing the 'darkness' of God's invisible Light and the 'darkness' of living by pure faith alone without the aid of sensible or intellectual vision. St. John took his basic illustration from the nature of physical light. A ray of sunlight streaming through the window is more noticeable when there are many particles of dust in the room on which the ray can reflect, but the fewer the particles of dust the more elusive and invisible the light is. Indeed if there were no particles of dust at all, and if the ray of light could come through one window and go out another without striking any material object, it would be completely invisible. The eye would have no images on which to rest, because the light itself is not the proper object of sight, but only the means through which visible things are seen.

This applies no less, St. John argued, to spiritual or supernatural Light which has a relation to the intellect, the eye of the soul, similar to the relation of natural light to the eye of the body. Here instead of particles of matter and sensible images we have to reckon with conceptual forms and mental images, thrown up by the discursive reason through its abstractive activity on sensible experience, which may interfere with the shining of supernatural Light, for they are creaturely representations and closed modes of thought which are apt to impede the Light and limit and obstruct our apprehension of divine Truth which is the proper object of spiritual knowledge. Hence some disciplined 'unknowing' of all that is inappropriate must take place if we are to open our minds to the purity of divine Light and Truth. This is the function of contemplative or mystical theology which, according to St. John, leads to the pure imageless knowing of faith that comes from the hearing of God's Word. All this is not to say that the habits of thought we develop in the various sciences are merely to be supplanted by supernatural or spiritual knowledge, for they may be taken up and transformed when united to that knowledge, much as a faint light which mingles with a bright light is not lost but sublimated and perfected even though it is not the light which supplies the prevailing and principal illumination. The Christian's concern, however, is not merely to advance in knowledge of intelligible, theological forms lit up by divine Light, so much as to know God himself who is the source of all illumination and whose invisibility infinitely surpasses the invisibility of physical light.

The difficulty that faces us in knowing God is the unapproachable or inaccessible nature of his divine Light, not the supposed fact, often put forward in the mystical tradition, that God is beyond all light and understanding, for God is wholly luminous and intelligible in himself and the ultimate Source of all light and intelligibility. This unapproachableness of God, as St. John of the Cross rightly understood it, is due to two reasons. (i) God is unapproachable because of the sheer invisibility of his uncreated Light, but that invisibility, unlike the invisibility of created light, is to be traced to the transcendence of his Light over our finite capacities. The higher and the more sublime the divine Light, the more inaccessible, the 'darker' it is to our intellect. It is thus the excess of divine Light over created light which, so to speak, puts God 'in the dark' for us, while the thickness of that darkness is in proportion to the infinite excess of his Light over ours. In Biblical language, by covering himself with Light as with a garment, God shrouds himself in a 'dark cloud' through which our minds cannot penetrate.   (ii) God is also unapproachable for us because of the inability of our impure minds to bear the sheer purity of his divine Light. The brighter the light, St. John observes, the more the owl is blinded and the more one looks at the blazing light of the sun, the more the sun darkens the faculty of sight, deprives and overwhelms it. But what overwhelms the sight of the sinner, is the utter holiness of God which consumes all his impurity and evil. Again, in Biblical language, God is a consuming fire; no one can see him and live. All this implies that actual knowledge of God by mankind may take place only (a) through the establishment of a reciprocity between God and man in which the uncreated Light of God adapts itself gently to the lowly understanding of our finite minds and at the same time through its creative touch elevates them to communion with God in such a way that they may have access to him beyond their creaturely capacities; and (b) through the accomplishment of reconciliation between man and God in which guilt is expiated, sin is forgiven and all its defilement is removed so that our minds may become clean like transparent windows through which there may stream the illuminating and transforming radiation of divine Light. Actual knowledge of God by way of such a two-fold relationship between God and man is mediated through the incarnation and passion of God's beloved Son in Jesus Christ. In him the invisible Light of God is made visible and, in indissoluble oneness with the eternal Word and Love of God, is made accessible to mankind 'through faith alone which comes by hearing' *(fides ex auditu)* — a doctrine which St. John of the Cross understood and expounded in a form which blended his pre-Reformation and post-Reformation emphases. There we must leave his thought.

The invisibility of physical light is a feature of nature which we now understand more fully. Even if light could stream into one window of a room and out of another without striking any particles of dust or any of the walls, the room would still be full of light for it would be reflected by the molecules of air through which it shone. Hence even in daytime those who fly at very high altitudes, where the air is thin and there are relatively few molecules of air to reflect the sun's luminous radiation, discover the sky to be a deep black. Actually light belongs to a range of luminous radiations in which it occupies a place between electromagnetic and infra-red radiations which have longer wave lengths and ultra-violet, x-ray and gamma radiations which have shorter wave lengths. All of them are quite invisible to us, for they move at such a speed that our human eyes cannot detect them, the speed of light. (It is only with the help of indirect means that we discover them). If we commonly speak of light as 'visible', it is not because it really is, but because the human eye is adapted to see, not the radiation itself, but its effect in lighting up whatever reflects it. I recall in this connection a visit I paid several years ago to a metereological station where photographs of the cloud cover over the earth were being received regularly from a man-made satellite. The concentrated stream of light signals conveying the information was quite invisible, but when I cut the stream with a sheet of paper immediately there appeared on it a spot of light : the invisible became indirectly visible. The visible spot of light was not the light itself, although it let us know that the light was there : it bore witness to the light which remained invisible in itself.

This is just how Irenaeus in the second century, recalling particularly the teaching of St. John's Gospel, spoke of the invisible God becoming visible in Jesus Christ. We may express this today by saying that in Jesus Christ God's own transcendent Light in personal and concentrated form has moved directly into the physical world of luminous phenomena created by him and become uniquely man within the contingent structures and objectivities and patterns of existence shaped and governed by the primacy of created light in the universe. As the creative Light of God incarnate he is 'the Light of the world', so that it is as we are enlightened by him that we may see light and come to know the invisible God. The incarnation, however, does not mean that Jesus Christ is just the unique spot of light in human existence where the concentrated beam of God's pure Light intersects it and is reflected by it, and where he merely bears witness to the presence of an invisible Light which he is not in himself. On the contrary, he is himself 'the real Light', as St. John called him. The incarnation is the actual embodiment of God's Light within the objective empirical realities of our world in such a way that Jesus Christ is acknowledged and worshipped as 'God of God and Light of Light', of one and the same being with the Light to which he bears witness. Thus he constitutes in the reality of his divine-human Person both the invisible radiation and the creaturely reflection of the eternal Light which God is. At the same time the incarnation of God's uncreated Light within the realm of created light does not involve in any way the overwhelming or swallowing up of created Light, but the very reverse : the assuming, confirming and finalising of the reality of created light in God himself, so that it is given a stability and a reliability beyond anything it could have by itself in its contingent nature. Thus in Jesus Christ we have contact, as St. Paul argued, not only with the image of the invisible God, but with him in whom, through whom, and unto whom all things were created, for he has priority over all and all things hold together in him.

By the incarnation, of course, is meant not just the irruption of God's eternal Light into our temporal existence or its once and for all embodiment within it, but the whole incarnate life of Jesus Christ saturated with the divine Light from his birth of the virgin Mary to his resurrection from the empty tomb. Jesus was completely and absolutely transparent with the Light of God. There was no darkness in him, nothing unreal, no deceit, no insincerity. He was utterly true and genuine, translucent with the sheer Truth of God himself, the one point in human existence where the divine Light shines through to the world purely and truly, unimpeded and unclouded by any distortion or refraction. Far from being less human because of that, he was more human than any other, indeed perfectly human, for with him the divine Light which is the source of all human life and light had its perfect way. He was so perfectly the man that he ought to have been that there was no gap in his nature resulting from a lapse from true humanity, as a result of which he was obliged to be what he was not but ought to be. The union between his human life and the humanising Light of the Creator was unbroken, so that it is through him that the eternal uncreated Light of God shines through to us.

Conversely expressed, Jesus was the life-giving Light of God translated into the form of a particular human life and at work among men precisely in its identity with that life. That is to say, Jesus was not just the most perfect man, the most human being that ever lived, shot through and through with divine Light, but God himself in his divine Light living among us as man. In, with and through Jesus the uncreated Light of God crossed the 'dark' barrier of his invisibility into our realm of created light and creaturely visibility, and at the same time penetrated into the great darkness of our rebellious self-alienation from God in which even the light that is in us has become darkness, in order to redeem us from its power and bring us into the Light of the divine Life. Thus regarded, the life of Jesus was much more than a human life alive with the Light of God. It was the living Light of God himself actively lived out among us as a human life, which continues to bear directly, personally, intimately upon the ontological depths of our human existence, searching, judging, cleansing, healing and renewing, and remains for ever the one light-bringing and life-giving Life for all mankind.

Now if the Life of Jesus is more than a reflection of God's invisible Light, but is that very Light incarnate in our human life and its created light, how are we to respond to it and apprehend it, for even as incarnate it retains its nature as Light? Let us recall that we cannot see physical light for it moves at such an incredible speed that our human eyes cannot detect it. The same applies to a bullet in flight which has a much slower speed, but if we could find a way of moving along with a bullet we would be able to see it. This would be quite impossible, of course, with physical light, the speed of which outstrips everything else in the universe, and yet it falls immeasureably short of the 'instantaneous' movement and action of divine Light! However, in translating his Light into the form of a human life in Jesus, God has adapted it to our human capacity and brought its motion within the range of our apprehension. Hence if we are to know and apprehend the Light of God incarnate in the life of Jesus Christ we must learn to move along with it and keep pace with it, and in fact become united to it in the course of its movement in our midst.

If physical light has anything to teach us here, it is that since light is never at rest but always in motion, in order to appreciate its nature and activity we must abandon any attempt to understand it from a point of absolute rest and develop an *a posteriori*, kinetic way of thinking in which we allow our minds to behave obediently in accordance with the movement of light and thereby penetrate into the intelligible relations and structures of the invisible space-time metrical field which controls all observable or visible realities in the empirical universe. With all relevant differences taken into account, it is surely a similar form of *a posteriori*, kinetic thought which is required if we are really to appreciate and understand the living Light which is the Life of Jesus Christ. Hence he summons us to uproot ourselves from all fixed preconceptions, to be yoked together with him and follow him in commitment to the way which he has taken in our alienated and darkened existence, not for his own sake but for our sakes. 'If any one will come after me, let him renounce himself and take up his cross and follow me.' 'I am the light of the world; he who follows me shall not walk in darkness, but shall have the light of life.' That is to say, we are called through a radical change of mind to live in obedient conformity to his embodiment of divine Light in our human being, and thus to follow him along the road which he has taken into the terrible darkness of the Cross where, however, he was not quenched by darkness for through the holiness of the life he lived and the death he died on our behalf he triumphed over it and through his resurrection from the grave he broke through the ultimate barrier of darkness and 'brought life and immortality to light'. Since it is in this enlightening and saving Life of the crucified and risen Jesus that the eternal Light and Life of God himself are mediated to us in a form in which we can share in death as well as life, it is through union and communion with Jesus that we are enabled to see the invisible God and live.

(3)   The last feature of light we are to consider is the relation of light to sound, or the discrepancy between light signals and sound signals which we may speak of as the *inaudibility* of light. But here we focus upon the analogical difference — which as Clerk Maxwell used to insist is always a point of capital importance — between created and uncreated light, for in its remarkable way God's Light is *audible light*. That is, God's Light has an intimate relation to his Word, to which we do not find any correspondence in nature. In the physical phenomena of nature, of course, there are auditory as well as luminous radiations, but auditory radiations or sound waves do not travel at anything like the speed of light — in fact they are extremely slow in comparison with it — so that sound does not have anything like the place of primacy in the universe that light has. At this point again we have to reckon with a fundamental difference, for God's Word does have along with his Light the place of absolute primacy in his relation to the universe he has made. God's Word and God's Light coinhere in one another and it is as such that they are the creative Source of all intelligibility in the universe.

Owing to its speed, physical light is the fastest messenger in the universe and as such constitutes the all-important link throughout empirical reality. Hence, as we have seen, it is through receiving and apprehending light signals that we may understand something of the spatio-temporal patterns of nature and even offer some account of the universe as a whole. Since these light signals are found to have mathematical properties we can give them numerate expression, but if we are properly to grasp what they signify, and communicate their meaning to others in the establishment of scientific knowledge, we have to translate the information that light signals carry into a form to which we can give verbal expression, much as we decode non-verbal messages signalled by morse or semaphore. That is to say, we require to decipher and interpret light signals through coordinating word with number if we are to grasp the message they convey and understand the specific nature of the universe they reveal. Only when the source-material of light is processed in this way can it be used as data on which to base scientific knowledge. In a hermeneutical process of this kind we are apt to import into our understanding of nature patterns of thought which derive from the socio-cultural deposit in the language we use, so that we need the regular discipline of checking our understanding of number with word in order to help us sieve away from our forms of thought and speech what is alien and irrelevant to the inquiry on which we are engaged, and to enable us to think as objectively about nature as we can. This interrelation between number and word is of not a little importance for theology and its relation to the determinate world of natural science, to which we must give fuller attention in the final chapter.

As we receive messages through light signals picked up by our radar telescopes from nebulae on the outermost boundaries of the universe millions and millions of light years away, we find ourselves in touch with the structures and patterns of the universe soon after it had come into being and as it continues in being, across the endless vastness of space and time. But these messages reach us in a mute and inarticulate form and require to be converted into word if we are to 'tune in' to them and 'hear' them, and grasp what they mean. It is otherwise with the message of God the Creator of the universe which we receive through the Light of his self-revelation to mankind, for it does not need to be converted into another form in order to be apprehended. It comes to us already in the form of Word, not to be sure, in the first instance at least, in the form of creaturely human word, but in the form of the eternal Word who inheres in the Being of God and is the ultimate creative Source of all 'word' or all capacity for speech, as God's Light is the ultimate creative Source of all light and vision. In God himself Light and Word are one and indivisible : his Light is his Word and his Word is his Light. Thus we may rightly think of God as revealing himself to us through *luminous Word* or *audible Light*.

Is this not how Jesus Christ the incarnate Son of God the Father is presented to us in the Fourth Gospel, in his identity as Word with the Light of God and his identity as Light with the Word of God, both in God himself and in his work of creation? He who has always dwelt with God, the Word who was what God was, became flesh and dwelt among us—and, St. John added, 'we beheld his radiance, the radiance of the only begotten from the Father'—full of grace and truth. No one has ever seen God, but the only begotten Son who belongs to the innermost being of the Father has made him known. That is to say, in Jesus Christ, the incarnate Son of God, the luminous Word or the audible Light of God himself, has become one with us in our human nature and condition in such a way as to be both the eternal Word of God and human word, both the uncreated Light of God and created light, in the indivisible unity of his life and person. God of God though he is, he has come not in the form of divine Majesty but in great humility as man, communicating and interpreting himself in human words and ways so that we who are human may hear and meet him. Man of man though he is, he has come not in a merely creaturely way but as the mighty Creator Word and Light of God, creatively calling forth from us the ability to have faith in him and the power to receive him as the very Word and Light of God into our human lives, and thereby to become children of God who are reborn in him. That is how the invisible Light of God still comes to us, audibly through the word of the Gospel, and is still appropriated through the hearing of faith, that is, in modes of human response which are in obedient conformity to the oneness of the Word and Light in God and in his self-revelation to mankind in Jesus Christ. In nature it is not sound but light that occupies a privileged place, but in grace it is faith rather than sight which is privileged. 'Blessed are they', said Jesus to St. Thomas, 'who have not seen and yet have believed.'

The Biblical view of the oneness of Word and Light in God himself and in his self-revelation to mankind, whether in the form it took in the Old Testament account of God's historical dialogue with Israel or in the form it took in the New Testament account of the incarnation of God's only begotten Son in Jesus Christ, has not had an easy passage in the history of theological thought. Serious problems have constantly cropped up in the great tradition which derives from St. Augustine and in his theology of illumination. These may be due in part to the primacy of light over sound in nature, which influenced Hellenic but not Hebraic thought, but they have a close connection with Augustine's epistemological dualism between the intelligible and sensible realms and his psychological approach to the understanding of Christian experience and doctrine, which threw the emphasis upon inward enlightenment or the vision of thought. In Jesus Christ, the incarnate Word or Wisdom of God, Light and Word were recognised as identical, but when he explained what this meant Augustine insisted that 'God speaks to us by illuminating us', and that while we may think of our illumination as a participation in the Word of God that means a participation in God's eternal Light. There is, in St. Augustine's thought, a corresponding relation in us between speech and sight or hearing and seeing. From a physical point of view locution and vision are different, but in the inward realm of our thoughts they are one and the same : the locutions or words of the mind are forms of vision or acts of insight, 'reflections conceived in the soul by divine Light.' 'That is why, although the outward speech is not seen but heard, the Holy Gospel can speak of the inward locutions which are thoughts as *seen* by our Lord and not heard'. Thus while word and light were regarded by St. Augustine as intrinsically one and the same in the realm of intelligible realities, whether in our inward mental life or in the life of God, word tended regularly to be resolved into light and communication into illumination. The primacy of light over word made it difficult in the last analysis to speak of 'word' except in some metaphorical sense in relation either to the vision of human thought or to the shining of divine Truth.

The difficulty became greater, not less, when Augustinian theology with its other-worldly spirituality was recast in abstractive Aristotelian terms, when the separation between the temporal and the eternal, the world and God, took on a harder form. On the one

hand, the notion of God as the Unmoved Mover
seriously damaged the understanding of divine interaction with the empirical world. 'God does not become
anything', as Peter Lombard expressed it—a conception of divine inertia which introduced lasting problems
into the doctrines of the incarnation and the real
presence. The shining of the divine Light across the
gap between God and the world was more conceivable
than the actual coming of a Word which eternally
inheres in the unchanging Being of God. On the other
hand, the intellectualist notion of word as formed by
the intellect in its union with the object to be the
vehicle of clear-cut concepts derived through the
reason, reinforced the need for contemplation which
strives for illumination beyond the grasp of reason and
which rises above the level of words and concepts to
reach the spiritual content and reality that transcend
them. Hence we find a very important place being
given to a form of Neoplatonic and Pseudo-Dionysian
'apophaticism' in which the human spirit 'takes-off', as
it were, in a wordless and conceptless mystical vision of
God. This was the misleading tendency in the theology
of illumination which St. Anselm sought to correct
when he insisted that behind all our understanding of
the rationalities of created existence and all divine
revelation to us through Holy Scripture we have to do
with an ultimate *speech* deep in the very Being of God
(intima locutio apud Summam Substantiam), and that
there can therefore be no knowledge of God except
through the conceptual relation of faith *(fides esse
nequit sine conceptione)*. It was this danger in mystical
theology which St. John of the Cross rather later sought
to counter in his emphasis upon audible light and the
hearing of faith.

How serious the problem had become in the
Augustinian-Thomist tradition of theology can be

indicated by reference to two points in the thought of St. Thomas Aquinas. First, to the question posed by Peter Lombard as to how God and the blessed converse with one another, St. Thomas gave the answer that they converse 'wordlessly' through intellectual vision alone. That is to say, when we pass beyond the realms of temporality into the realm of eternal intelligible undifferentiated Light, the kind of communication which we have with one another in the world, and with God in the pilgrimage of the Church on earth, through the mediation of word, falls away and is replaced by the timeless immediate communication of the beatific vision. Secondly, while admitting that in our case as creaturely beings in time understanding *(intelligere)* and speaking *(dicere)* are interconnected, St. Thomas claimed that this cannot be said of God. Hence he consistently criticised St. Anselm's view that there is a distinct speaking *(dicere)* as well as understanding *(intelligere)* or a profound speech *(locutio)* inherent in the Being of God. That meant for St. Anselm, as it had meant for the Nicene theology of St. Athanasius or St. Hilary, that God's Being is intrinsically eloquent and not mute for his Word dwells essentially in him, and that in his self-revelation to us in Word God speaks to us in Person, communicating to us not just something about himself but his very Self, as is made clear in the incarnation of his eternal Word in the Person of Jesus Christ. In that event the concept of *word* in the Holy Scripture through which God's self-revelation to us in the Holy Scripture continues to be mediated, must be taken quite realistically, so that, if we are to be consistent, we may not treat the Holy Scripture in such a way that through some kind of oblique or allegorical interpretation we merely use it as a base from which to take off into a transcendental realm of wordless communion with God in Light.

It is worth noting in this connection the remarkable protest against the Augustinian-Thomist notion of the Word made by John Reuchlin at the end of the fifteenth century, in which he put his finger on the crux of the problem when he opposed a realist Hebraic to a Hellenic understanding of word and appealed to the teaching of the Nicene Creed in respect of the 'consubstantial' relation between Jesus Christ and God the Father Almighty. If Jesus Christ is of one and the same being with God as incarnate Son that must apply to him also as incarnate *Word* of God. That is to say, what God is toward us in his self-revelation in Jesus Christ as the Word made flesh, he is in his own divine Being, so that it must be acknowledged that the Word dwells eternally in God *as Word*. If Jesus Christ is not very God of very God, being of one substance with the Father, if there is no final identity in being and act between Jesus Christ the Word made flesh and the eternal Word of God, then there is no ultimate consistency in the Gospel, for all that Jesus Christ revealed to us of God the Father and all that he did for us and for our salvation, would have no ultimate ground or validity in the eternal Reality of God. John Reuchlin was surely right, therefore, about the crucial importance of the consubstantial relation between Jesus Christ and God the Father, which is so central to the Nicene Faith, for if that relation does not hold in reality, it would mean that God is utterly unrelated to and indifferent to our human condition and has no place or time for us in his unchanging Being. If that relationship is not acknowledged, we would be forced to admit that the love of Jesus Christ proclaimed in the Gospel is not anchored in divine Reality and that God does not so love us that he gave his only begotten Son to be the Saviour of the world. Here, then, we are brought back to belief in the utter constancy, invariance, faithfulness, or truth of God in all his relations toward us, which we found to be disclosed in the activity and nature of God's eternal Light. The very Light of God could not be consistently Light, and certainly could not be known as such, if Jesus Christ were not also Word of Word as well as Light of Light, and thus immutably, eternally God of God as both Light and Word.

+ + + + +

BOOKS RELEVANT TO THIS CHAPTER

A. EINSTEIN.

Relativity. The Special and the General Theory. Tr. by R. W. Lawson. Crown Publishers, New York, 1961.

A. EINSTEIN, H. A. LORENTZ, H. WEYL, H. MINKOWSKI.

The Principle of Relativity. A Collection of the Original Memoirs on the Special and General Theory of Relativity, with notes by A. Sommerfeld. Tr. by W. Perrett and G. B. Jeffrey. Dover Publications, New York, 1952.

H. BONDI.

Relativity and Common Sense. A New Approach to Einstein. Heinemann, London, 1965.

MAX BORN.

The Born-Einstein Letters. Tr. by Irene Born. Macmillan, London, 1971.

LOUIS DE BROGLIE.

Physics and Microphysics. Foreword by A. Einstein. Harper Torchbooks, New York, 1960.

E. H. HUTTEN.

The Ideas of Physics. Oliver and Boyd, Edinburgh, 1967.

M. R. COHEN and I. E. DRABKIN.

A Source Book in Greek Science. McGraw-Hill, New York, 1948.

S. SAMBURSKY.

The Physical World of Late Antiquity. Routledge and Kegan Paul, London, 1962.

V. LOSSKY.

The Image and Likeness of God. St. Vladimir's Seminary Press, Crestwood, New York, 1974.

ST. JOHN OF THE CROSS.

Collected Works. Tr. by K. Kavanaugh and O. Rodriguez. Thomas Nelson, London, 1966.

A. H. ARMSTRONG (editor).

The Cambridge History of Later Greek and Early Medieval Philosophy. Cambridge University Press, Cambridge, 1976.

R. H. NASH.

The Light of the Mind. St. Augustine's Theory of Knowledge. The University Press of Kentucky, Lexington, 1969.

T. F. TORRANCE.

Theological Science. Oxford University Press, London, 1969.

Theology in Reconciliation. Geoffrey Chapman, London, 1975.

4.

Word and Number

We have found that the physical universe as it came from the creative intention and power of God is essentially a universe of light, for it is ordered throughout in accordance with the primacy of light and its invariant behaviour, but if its inherent rational order is to be understood it must be brought to coordinate expression in mathematical and verbal terms. The light signals which reach us from all over the universe, from its sub-atomic to its astrophysical dimensions, are message-laden radiations which require mathematical representation and description if they are to be received, let alone grasped, for what they are. These light signals are not just bare physical facts but are physical facts configured to coherent and significant patterns by means of which they convey, beyond what they are in themselves, information about the universe which requires to be appropriately expressed if it is to be grasped. Since it is in the reference of these patterns to what takes place in the universe that their meaning lies, we try not only to give mathematical expression to those patterns, but to discern and articulate the meaning disclosed through that reference, which may be done only through the medium of language. Thus through the combination of language and mathematics we seek to allow light signals to speak for themselves out of their information content and to interpret for us the message that they convey about the universe.

This interaction of number and word, however, is all-important for our understanding and interpretation not only of luminous phenomena but of all realities and events in the physical creation, for thereby their manifold order becomes accessible to conceptualisation and formalisation. In number we have to do with the rationality of the creation in its impersonal, determinate and immanent form. Hence in our scientific investigation of the physical world we do not reckon that we have made significant contact with the nature of things or grasped them in the depth of their reality unless we can bring our knowledge of them to a clear, consistent and enlightening mathematical represent-ation. At the same time we are aware that our mathe-matical equations are meaningful only in so far as they bear upon non-mathematical objective reality in-dependent of them. Hence the physicist is concerned with mathematical formalisations not just as consistent sets of abstract symbols or axioms but with the connect-ion between them and the actual realities he is investig-ating, i.e. with the openness of mathematical structures to ontological structures in the real world beyond them. Through mathematics he is able to use a notation that carries his reasoning beyond what he is capable of without it, but it requires to be applied to reality. That is to say, without interpretation of its extra-mathematical, empirical reference, mathematical formalisation can tell us nothing about the universe.

In word we have to do with the rationality of the creation in its personal form in which it transcends the visible and tangible levels of its impersonal, determinate and immanent condition. Through interaction with word the orderly connections in nature to which we give mathematical formalisation are found to be incomplete in themselves, but are coordinated with orderly connections of a wider and richer kind at higher levels of reality from which they gain a meaning and consistency which they could not have if confined to themselves. Thus through the interpretative function of language mathematical formalisations of determinate and tangible states of affairs are not allowed to become pointless abstract symbolic systems but are applied to serve forms of rationality that transcend them.

Both forms of rationality, number and word, are needed in order to understand the tangible and intangible levels of reality. Different though they are they come together in man, in the interrelation and inseparability of his physical and spiritual existence in space and time, and they operate together in the ongoing expansion of the universe as it is explored and developed through man's interaction with nature and as its inherent rationality is brought to coordinate expression in mathematical and verbal language. The emergence of scientific knowledge is not something alien to the creation, imposed upon it *ab extra,* but is part of its proper development and thus a manifestation of its inherent nature and intelligibility, but it is through man and his handling of number and word that this takes place. Just as the creation is given to produce life of itself, so it is given to produce its own self-articulation and thus to rise above its mute and confined condition. This takes place through man, 'the crown and priest of creation', who is the intelligent constituent of the universe whereby it comes to know itself and express its God-given intelligibility, and the child of God created in his own image through whom the creation is ordained to serve the transcendent purpose and unlimited freedom of the Creator.

In all this process word and number, number and word, necessarily interact with one another. Number cannot come to expression, nor can it be consistently

and meaningfully handled, apart from the interpretative and controlling function of word, for it is through
coordination with verbal formalisations that mathematical formalisations are applied to empirical reality
on the one hand and are integrated with wider and
richer intelligible connections on the other hand,
without either of which mathematics would be no more
than a mere game. At the same time it must be pointed
out that word cannot fulfil its role apart from number,
that is, without the realm of the determinate and the
invariant which supplies the reliable medium for the
development of intelligible systems of representation
and therefore the underpinning that is needed for
universality and continuity in communication. Words
have a tendency to take off on their own in which case
they become arbitrary and nonsensical, and require to
function within the constraints and distraints of the
empirical or physical levels of reality and their
determinate connections if their own operations are
not to fail.

From this perspective alone, that is, of the mutual
interrelation of number and word, it becomes evident
that natural science and theological science have not a
little in common, at least so far as the intellectual
aspect of each is concerned. There are of course great
differences between them in respect of the particular
objective to which each is devoted and the nature of the
subject into which each inquires. It is the aim of
natural science to investigate the empirical world, that
is, the realm of created realities in their utter different-
iation from God, which are to be appreciated and
understood out of their contingent nature and
intelligibility and therefore out of their natural
processes alone without taking God into account. It is
the aim of theological science to inquire into the ways
and works of God as they are made known through his

divine self-revelation to mankind, and through them all to worship and know God in his utter distinctness from all that he has made, without projecting into our knowledge of him creaturely images or representations of any kind. However, even when natural science is able to offer a convincing rational account of the marvellous order and harmony of any field of nature or indeed of the universe as a whole, it must still ask over and above all that what the sufficient reason for this rational state of affairs is, for it is aware that the rationality inherent in the universe with which it has made contact reaches far beyond the range of its competence. In other words, through the coordination of number-rationality and word-rationality a transcendent element presses upon the scientific reason in such a way that questions are roused within its inquiry which knock on the gates of the ultimate intelligible Ground of the universe, and they are questions which blend with those asked in theological inquiry. Theological science on the other hand, even when it is able to offer an appropriate and enlightening account of the intelligible self-communication of God to us in Jesus Christ his incarnate Word, must ask questions about the structured objectivities of the world of space and time within which the incarnation took place and through which God continues to make himself known to us by his Word. That is to say, theological inquiry is unable to give serious attention to the Word which God has addressed to man without taking into account the determinate objectivities and intelligibilities of the created order with which it is clothed and through which it always is mediated to us. Therein, however, theological inquiry bears upon the rational connections inherent in the empirical world which natural science seeks to bring to mathematical representation and description. Thus questions rising out of theological science are found to blend with questions asked in the inquiries of natural science.

We have seen that the way in which natural science and theological science both coordinate the rationalities of number and word in the development of their inquiries and the formulation of their results leads them to raise basic questions which have an area of overlap. What is at stake in and behind all that is a common concern for objectivity and truth in the fundamental basis of human knowledge. They both presuppose that there is an objective rationality in the field of their inquiry which has an unconditional claim upon their recognition, and that truth is not invented but discovered for it becomes disclosed to them as something over which they have no control. Both natural science and theology coordinate number and word in such a way as to sustain this twofold commitment to objectivity and truth, but they do it in different ways.

While the main interest of scientific knowledge of the physical world, in accordance with its determinate nature, must be in the handling of number, this requires to be coordinated with the use of word precisely in order to apply mathematical formalisation to objective reality, and thereby to avoid the slide of mathematics into empty formalism. This is a temptation to which mathematics is constantly subjected through its abstract symbolic character and its tendency to engage in idealising generalisations. But since the physicist, as Richard Feynman has pointed out, is not interested in the general but in the special case, he insists on translating into language what he has figured out in his mathematics so that it may bear upon the actualities of nature with which he is experimenting. It is thus in and through the connection of words with the real world that he maintains his orientation to objective reality.

The main interest of the theologian, on the other hand, in accordance with the personal and intangible nature of his subject-matter, falls upon word or *logos,* for through his inquiries he seeks to understand an objective rationality which may be expressed appropriately in and through language. Theological articulation, however, because of its conceptual and linguistic character, easily slides into an empty formalism detached from objective reality, unless it operates on the ground of God's actual self-revelation to us in and through the created order of the world in which he has placed us and in which he has incarnated his Word. Since theology is interested, not in some kind of speculative 'knowledge' of God behind his back, as it were, but in real knowledge of God in accordance with the way he has taken in making himself known to us in the created order, the theologian must clarify the relation of his thought and language to the spatio-temporal structures and continuities of the created order, and allow the determinate forms of objectivity and intelligibility they enshrine to exercise appropriate constraint over all his formulations. Thus it is in and through persistent attention to the empirical correlates of theological knowledge, which are subject to under-standing and interpretation through number, that the theologian may maintain his orientation to objective reality.

It follows from the common concern of natural science and theological science with objective rational-ity and reality that they are also concerned to recognise that truth is not invented but discovered. It is to be granted, of course, that in theology as well as in natural science knowledge is not acquired in some sort of packaged form, but is gained only through intelligent interaction between us and the reality into which we inquire, whether that be nature or God. In natural science, for example, we have to 'invent' geometries and creatively work out patterns of thought, but we do so under the compulsion of patterns embodied in nature such as we find already to hand in crystalline formations. Likewise we interact with nature through controlled experimental questioning in order to get answers which nature does not spontaneously hand to us, as it were, on a plate. Nevertheless we put our questions to nature not in accordance with pre-conceived stipulations which would only yield pre-determined answers, but in such a way that we allow our questions to be constantly revised in accordance with what nature tells us about itself, for we recognise that nature itself is the ultimate judge of the truth or falsity of our concepts and statements about it. *Mutatis mutandis,* all this applies equally to theological inquiry. In theological science we have to 'invent' terms and concepts and creatively work out doctrinal patterns of thought, such as we have in the Nicene-Constantinopolitan Creed, but they represent what the Church found itself compelled to think and say on the ground of God's self-revelation in Jesus Christ. It is through constant interaction with God's self-revelation in the continuing worship and mission of the Church that we learn to frame appropriate questions in theological inquiry and to formulate our understanding in the light of the answers given, in the conviction that God alone through his Word is the final Judge of the truth or falsity of our thought and speech about him, and therefore in the conviction that all the answers we formulate are revisable, for their truth does not lie in themselves but in the realities to which they refer, independent of themselves.

It is important, however, to note the difference that obtains between natural science and theological science in this respect, which relates to the nature of the

realities with which each is concerned. The kind of
rationality embedded in physical nature, as we have
seen, is amenable to mathematical treatment and
formulation, that is, in terms of number. But the kind
of rationality which we encounter in God's acts of
revelation and salvation in Jesus Christ his incarnate
Word is not amenable to quantifying treatment or
formulation, but in accordance with its intrinsically
articulate nature it is to be understood and expressed in
terms of word. While number and word require to be
correlated with one another if each is to retain its
distinctive character and fulfil its proper function in
our knowledge, to confuse them with one another
would be tantamount to a category mistake of a very
grave order. Now when we take into account this basic
difference in the nature of the object and its specific
form of rationality we find that we have to draw a
distinction between the ways in which we learn the
truth in natural and in theological inquiry. We may
characterise this as a distinction between *discovery* and
revelation.

In natural science authentic learning is an act of
sheer discovery, that is, not the inferring of some
additional piece of knowledge from what we already
know, but a forward leap of the mind in apprehending
what is radically new and which we could only learn
out of itself. We talk about interrogating nature in
order to let it disclose itself, reveal itself or even declare
itself to us, but that is metaphorical language, for
actually nature is mute or dumb. We have to devise
ways—physical experiments—in which we put our
questions to nature but we must also formulate the
answers nature gives us through its reaction to
experiments. All this is heavily controlled so that we
may not read into nature what is not there, that is,
so that we may not substitute our own conceptual

creations for patterns of thought which nature itself imposes on our minds. Thus we take pains to preserve the heuristic nature of scientific discovery.

In theological science authentic learning is also an act of sheer discovery, for we are not concerned with projecting into God what we already know of ourselves, but with learning something about God which is radically new to us. Here, however, we engage not with a mute or dumb reality (that would be an idol) but with One who freely acts upon us and addresses us in his Word, thereby disclosing, revealing or declaring himself to us, in a proper sense, through an articulate mode of communication. We learn what is new through listening to it, and letting ourselves be told what we could never tell ourselves. Thus we are concerned in theological inquiry not just with discovery but with God's own initiative in active self-revelation in an articulate and intelligible form. This is an information-laden communication which does not need to be 'decoded' or 'unscrambled' into some other form in order to be apprehended or expressed, for it reaches us as real Word from God addressed to us in the communicable form of word with which we are already familiar in our human inter-personal relations. We do not need to discuss the fact that the uncreated Word of God, unlike our creaturely word, is not separate from his personal Being as Speaker, and that as such it is not less than what we understand by 'word' but infinitely more, as became clear in the incarnation of God's Word in Jesus Christ in whom God communicated not just something about himself but his very Self to us. The point to be stressed here is that in theological inquiry we have to reckon not simply with discovery but with revelation in the proper sense as an articulate and intelligible form of real communication. While this is mediated to us through the created objectivities and intelligibilities of our spatio-temporal existence, and therefore in the specific modes of our human thought and speech, it is addressed to us by God himself from the ultimate ground and under the creative control of his transcendent Objectivity and Intelligibility. Thus while theological inquiry is a very human enterprise in which we pray, we ask questions, we learn, and we formulate, all our authentic knowing of God takes shape under the commanding revelation and lordly authority of God himself. As Karl Barth used to say, God remains 'indissolubly Subject' even when he is the Object of our learning and discovery.

In any wide-ranging discussion of the interrelation of word- and number-rationality in human knowledge, we should not forget the fact which we noted somewhat earlier that there are other basic modes of rationality, notably those with which we have to do in the biological sciences and the fine arts. Organismic form and aesthetic form are, I believe, modes of rationality in their own proper right which demand serious consideration. They belong to the complex manifold of rationality in the universe, contributing in various ways to the overall structure and character of nature, but also to the interrelations of word and number which we have been considering, as well as participating in those modes of rationality. We are unable to explore here the fascinating complex which such a combination of rational modalities involves for our understanding of the created order or of our relations with God the creative Source of all form and beauty in the universe. Our immediate purpose is rather limited : to draw out some of the implications of the relationship between word and number for Christian theology, in which word is certainly to be accorded the primary place, but in which number, as we have been thinking of it in connection with the determinate aspect of the created order, has a significant if subsidiary contribution to make.

(1) The contingency of word and number

In an early work, *Tractactus Logico-Philosophicus*, Ludwig Wittgenstein examined the relation between words and things in any language and contended for something in common between the structure of a sentence and the structure of the fact it asserted. Whether that particular thesis holds or not, Wittgenstein felt that we have to understand these questions against the background of the contingent nature of the world which to be what it is depends upon a non-contingent factor of intrinsic meaning and worth beyond it. 'The meaning of the world', he claimed, 'must lie outside of it. In the world everything is as it happens, in it there is no worth — and if there were, it would have no worth. If there is any worth that does have worth, it must lie outside all that happens and is the case. For all that happens and is the case is contingent. What makes it non-contingent cannot lie *in* the world, for otherwise it would also be contingent. It must lie outside the world.' It is not clear from this passage whether Wittgenstein was working with the Judaeo-Christian concept of contingence, or with the traditional idea, derived from Hellenic thought, of the contingent as the merely accidental or irrational in contrast to what is necessary or rational, or perhaps with the Kantian refinement of that in which the contingent refers not to what happens by mere chance but to what is ultimately conditioned by necessity. At any rate, the general notion is that since contingent things do not have to be and contingent events do not have to happen, once they are or do happen, they are what they are and have to be appreciated through their dependence on something else of independent, self-sufficient reality with intrinsic rationality or worth.

From the perspective of Christian theology which has radicalised the concept of contingence, the contingent nature of the world and of its order is to be understood from the constitutive relation between God and the universe which he has freely, but not without reason, created out of nothing, and to which he has given a distinctive existence of its own. utterly different from God's, which he loves, preserves and respects. Therein God has conferred upon the creation and continues to sustain an authentic reality and integrity and a genuine order of its own which must be respected by us also, for while the contingent universe is neither self-sufficient nor self-explanatory it is given a rationality and a reliability in its orderly empirical reality which depend on and reflect God's own eternal rationality and reliability. The baffling thing about the contingent nature of the world and its rational order, is the inter-locking of dependence and independence which it implies. The independence of the universe depends entirely upon the free creative act of God to give it being and form wholly differentiated from himself, but this is an independence that is conditioned by the dependence which anchors the universe beyond itself in the reality and freedom of the Creator. It is to be firmly noted that the radical distinction between uncreated and created being, between the uncreated Rationality of God and the created rationality of the world, far from reducing the being and rationality of the contingent world to unreality and insignificance, establishes their reality and secures their significance, not in spite of, but precisely in their contingent nature.

On the one hand, then, the contingence of the universe and its rational order implies that the universe as a whole and in all its constituent features, patterns and laws, has an autonomous character that must be respected, so that everything that takes place within it must be investigated in accordance with its natural right and integrity. On the other hand, however, the contingence of the universe and its rational order implies that nothing going on in the universe can be finally understood or explained in terms of universal laws or necessary truths immanent in the universe, for the deepest secret of the universe lies outside its own contingent reality. In other words, the universe instead of being closed in upon itself constitutes an open system with an ontological and intelligible reference beyond its own limits to an ultimate Ground of being and rationality upon which it depends for the internal consistency of its structure and order.

Now it is within this constitutive but radically contingent relation between God and the universe, which he has established and continues to maintain through his creative Word, that we are to interpret the role of word and number, as forms of contingent rationality which answer to the uncreated transcendent Rationality of God. This puts a distinctive theological slant upon our understanding both of 'the book of nature' and 'the book of God', that is, upon the language of creation and the language of the Bible which, in their different ways, we may read as articulating the speech of God.

In the biblical tradition the laws of the created order were thought of as soundlessly and voicelessly echoing the commanding speech of the Creator. Considered in themselves we regard natural laws today as economic descriptions of autonomous normative structures in the universe. We discover them with great effort through empirico-theoretical scientific inquiry and seek to bring them to expression through the combination of number and word, but we do not pretend that we can do more than reach provisional formalisations of them, far less that we can offer ultimate reasons for them. In this event the old notion that natural laws are divine forms or timeless necessities immanently embodied in nature falls away completely, and in their place we have a more dynamic and open-structured yet more objective conception of natural law, which is much more congenial to our theological outlook. In accordance with the biblical tradition we speak of the rise of natural law under the creative address of God's Word which summons the processes of the contingent world into orderly and antiphonal response. Thus there is generated throughout the universe a creaturely correspondence, a contingent language answering obediently to the Voice of the Creator. Natural laws, therefore, may be regarded as empirical sequences and regularities, symmetries and invariant relations which God has imparted to nature amidst all the changes and varieties of its contingent processes, but what they ultimately are as *laws* they are by reference to the legislative Word and unifying Rationality of God the Creator and Sustainer of the universe. Thus from a theological perspective the underlying connection, the ultimate consistency, in natural laws is grounded beyond their limits in God's creative upholding of the contingent universe 'by the word of his power', thereby anchoring it in the constancy and reliability of his own eternal Reality as God. It is because in this way the universe in its contingent nature and rationality is ceaselessly maintained as the created counterpart to the inexhaustible Nature and unlimited Rationality of God, that it is characterised throughout not by a static but by a dynamic stability, not by closed rigid structures but by open-ordered structures, not by necessary truths of reason but by contingent truths which defy complete mathematical formalisation.

When we turn from considering the language of creation to consider the language of divine revelation we do not move out of the realm of contingent existence and rationality where consistent natural laws obtain, for this is the realm to which we ourselves belong, and it is to us only within this realm that God addresses himself. Here, however, we have to reckon not just with the mute number-language of the physical creation but with an articulate and personal form of divine self-communication, in which the eternal Word of God has taken creaturely and human form in order to address us and be heard and understood by us *as word*. This takes place through the medium of our thought and speech which is no less contingently related to God than the physical creation. This is precisely what we find in the incarnation. In Jesus Christ the Creator Word of God, who is quite independent of all that he has freely called into being, freely became man himself within the conditions, objectivities and intelligibilities of contingent human existence, unreservedly assimilating them to himself and making them his own, in order as man to address mankind in the personal articulate form of contingent human word or thought and speech.

Let me cite at this point what I have written elsewhere, in *God and Rationality*. 'Now the Word of God did not enter this sphere of created rationality as a stranger, for in the incarnation he came to his own, but he did enter into what was creaturely and contingent and therefore utterly different : and this *difference* must be taken into account. In the Creator himself, Word, Person and Act are one and undivided, but in the creature they fall apart. With us word is different from act. We speak, but have to exert additional power in order to fulfil what we say in deeds. We act, but our acts are not personal in themselves. Our speech and

our action do not coincide in the unity and power of
our person. Act and person, word and person, word
and act are all separate — they are not unrelated, but
their relationship is conditioned by physical existence
and is refracted and strung out in time. With God it is
not so. He encounters us as One whose Word and whose
Act belong to the self-subsistence of his Person. What
he speaks takes place of itself, for it is filled with the
power of his Person, the power by which he is what he
is and by which he lives his own personal Life in
absolute self-sufficiency and freedom. His power to act
is none other than the power of his Person or the power
of his Word. He is in Person identical with his Word,
and his Word is itself his Act. However, when the
Word of God condescended to participate in created
existence in order to become Word to man, personally
addressing him in the medium of human speech and
physical event in space and time, he entered into the
divided and finite condition of word, person and act
and into the duality of number and word, that
characterised created reality. He came as genuine man,
physically conditioned in space and time, in whom
willing, speaking and doing are different, who thinks
and forms judgements, whose acts follow upon his
decisions, whose words are in addition to his person and
whose works are in addition to his words, but who in
none of these things is self-sufficient, for as man he lives
and thinks and speaks and acts only in inseparable
relation to his fellow-men and in dependence upon the
physical creation. Clearly, for the eternal Word of God
to become understandable and communicable in the
mode and character of word to man he had to share to
the full in the space-time distinctions and connections
of human existence in this world and operate within
the finite conditions of created rationality. This is not
to say, of course, that he ceased to be the Word of God

he is in the Creator, but rather that he appropriated human form within the frame of earthly life and action and speech in such a way as to take up the frail finite conditions of the creature into himself not merely as the earthen vessel of the Word of God but as his actual speaking of it to us. In Jesus Christ the Word has become physical event in space and time, meets us in the indissoluble connection of physical and spiritual existence, and is to be understood within the coordinate levels of created rationality. The unity in God between Person, Word and Act has been made to overlap and gather within its embrace the difference between person, word and act in the creature, so that they are allowed to mediate God's Word to man in time through a oneness between Christ's human utterance about God and God's self-utterance to man.' In the union between God and man in the one Person of Jesus Christ there is included a union not only of uncreated Light and created light, uncreated Rationality and created rationality, but of uncreated Word and created word, yet in such a way that the contingent word of man instead of being overwhelmed or diminished is taken up into the speaking of the divine Word in which it is perfected as human word through God's creative power and for ever established in the ultimate Reality of God himself. Therein Jesus Christ the Word made flesh becomes God's unique and exclusive language to mankind and he alone must be our proper human language to God.

In the following section of this chapter, we shall have to consider what happens when the language of creation and the language of revelation are split apart or one is given an improper ascendancy over the other. But now let us try to draw together our discussion of number-language and word-language to show how in being harnessed together each contributes to our knowledge of objective rationality in the contingent universe and of God in such a way that we are committed to the creative authority of truth independent of ourselves.

Since the Word of God comes to us within the spatio-temporal structures of the on-going empirical world in which we live and which is creatively and consistently upheld by his divine power, it is all-important for theology to respect the integrity and significance of the contingent universe as it becomes disclosed through the activities of natural science, for otherwise we would fail to respect the Word of God himself and would fail to do justice to the authenticity of his self-utterance to us in Jesus Christ. Since it is within the concrete objectivities of our creaturely existence in the world that the Word of God has freely objectified himself for us, thus making his divine Objectivity overlap with ours, assuming it into his own and thereby reinforcing it, it is within that overlap alone that we may have genuinely objective knowledge of God. In this way the stubborn, consistent objectivity of empirical reality, which in natural science we learn to acknowledge and respect for what it is independent of our knowing of it, plays a divinely given role in the service of God's self-revelation to us and correspondingly in the service of our objective knowledge of him.

The creaturely objectivity with which we have to do in knowledge of God is not any creaturely objectivity or just creaturely objectivity in general but that specific creaturely objectivity which the divine Objectivity assumed, adapted and bound to himself, Jesus. In him the Word of God has addressed himself to us in the intelligible forms of human thought and speech, and therefore in the articulate medium of verbal communication. In him we hear the Word of God directly addressing us in human words which we may understand only in accordance with the semantic and syntactic functions and structures of human language, but in him we meet the one indivisible Word of God himself who does not disappear behind the words through which he speaks to us, far less is he resolvable into them, for he remains the Word who eternally inheres in and is indissolubly one with the Personal Being of God himself. Thus the Word has eternal Objectivity in God's own Being *as Word,* for God eternally utters and expresses himself in his Word and is himself the Reality of his Word. It is to that ultimate Objectivity of the Word in the infinite depth of the Being and Reality of God that the human words appropriated and adapted by God for his self-communication to mankind go back, and it is through being grounded upon it that they have their objective truth and compelling claim upon our acknowledgment in the hearing of faith. That is why the Truth with which we are concerned in Christian theology is nothing less than the Being of God which is also his Word, and the Word of God which is also his Personal Being. In all our interpretation of the words of God's self-revelation mediated to us in the Holy Scriptures and in all our theological understanding and formulation, everything depends ultimately upon the *creative speaking* of God which is the ground of all true knowledge of him, the source of our ability to speak of him, and the active guide to all our understanding and inquiry of him in his self-revelation. It is because all contingent realities in the form of number or word have their final truth in God's Word rather than in themselves, that in their employment by the Word himself they may serve the communication to us of a knowledge of God that is quite beyond us. But because these created realities which God uses as the medium of his communication have their final truth in his Word rather than in themselves, they are in themselves far different from what they are in our knowledge and formalisation of them, so that instead of trying to reach knowledge of God through our speculative reasoning from created realities, we must let them fulfil for us the denotative function they are given in God's Word, i.e. to point above and beyond themselves to God's own Truth and Reality.

(2) **Equilibrium in the framework of knowledge**

This is a theme to which we have already had to give a lot of attention at various stages in the argument of this book. It came up when we discussed the dualist disjunction between the empirical and theoretical ingredients in knowledge and the transition to a unitary framework of thought which came especially with relativity theory. It also came before us in the second chapter when we noted the significance of Clerk Maxwell's stress on 'embodied mathematics' and the unfruitful knowledge of nature that crops up when the mathematical and experimental approaches are not integrated, but also the significance of his warning against 'partial explanations' to which we are prone in our recourse to abstractions and artificial mechanical models of thought. Our purpose now is not to go over that ground, but in view of the immediately preceding discussion on the bearing of number and word upon one another to point up what happens when some form of disequilibrium is allowed to intrude itself into the firmament of theological knowledge.

There is much to be said in favour of the thesis, recently advanced in a fresh way by the American physicist Richard Schlegel, that physics is the most important of the liberal arts, for it defines the general framework in which all the liberal arts are pursued and indeed the basic structure on which we build our civilisation. After all it is the physical world which sets the stage of our human drama, he argues, and what is more 'it places virtually absolute conditions on what we may believe or do'. These conditions were certainly very restrictive so far as the rigid mechanical determinism advocated by Pièrre Simon de Laplace was concerned, since it had no place within its framework of explanation for the freedom and the conscious mind of the scientist himself! However, that narrow dogmatic outlook has now given place, not least in the face of quantum physics, to a non-determinist outlook in which 'we no longer are obliged to think of nature as having set our future path', for we work with a new 'conception of nature forming itself as events occur'. 'We can think, then, not of the world fulfilling a predetermined pattern, but instead of its establishing what it is as it develops.' Even so, Richard Schlegel recognises that physics, like all the natural sciences, can offer only a highly partial and a highly fragmentary account of the universe, so that it needs to be balanced by other liberal arts, and not least, I would add, by theological science, if we are to reach a proper wholeness or equilibrium in our understanding of the universe and man's place within it.

Here, then, is the persistent dilemma on the horns of which our dualistically based European culture has been impaled again and again, particularly since Sir Isaac Newton produced his immensely powerful and successful 'system of the world' : natural science or the humanities. This has often been the choice between accepting the dominance of a determinate frame of thought grounded on the causal structures of the physical universe and an indeterminate frame of reference centred in the socio-personalistic structures of human existence and activated by the creative subjectivity of the human spirit. Frequently, however,

the choice has degenerated into one between a rationalistic scientism and an irrational romanticism, or an
objectivist positivism and a subjectivist existentialism,
although, strange as it may seem, these extremes not
infrequently pass over into each other.

So far as Christian theology is concerned, history
shows that in the last three hundred years it has been
trapped fairly regularly in the various forms of this
dilemma, which is admittedly understandable in view
of the Augustinian-Newtonian outlook within which it
has taken shape. Generally speaking two contrasting
orientations have tended to emerge. On the one hand,
under the dominance of the mathematico-physical
outlook, a determinate pattern of thought has been
allowed to gain an unbalanced ascendancy, for
example, in Protestant scholasticism or in present-day
'process theology'. On the other hand, in reaction to
the encroaching power of physical science and its
classical causalism, an indeterminate frame of thought
has been allowed to gain an ascendancy, for example,
in Protestant pietism or in the retreat of liberal theology
into a fuzzy realm of 'poetic' or 'oblique' truth. It will
be sufficient for our purpose here to examine, as 'test
cases', the Calvinistic doctrine of divine predestination
and the modern liberal doctrine of a non-conceptual or
non-cognitive relation to God.

(a) *Election or predestination.* Properly regarded,
divine election is the free sovereign decision and utterly
contingent act of God's Love in pure liberality or unconditional Grace whether in creation or in redemption.
As such it is neither arbitrary nor necessary, for it flows
freely from an ultimate reason or purpose in the
invariant Love of God and is entirely unconditioned by
any necessity, whether of being or knowledge or will, in
God and entirely unconstrained and unmotivated by
anything whatsoever beyond himself. What we cannot

understand is *why*, but here we have to do with the
relation between the uncreated Rationality of God and
the created rationality of our world and so with the
divine reason for election which lies hidden deep
behind all the reasonableness of the created order. In
so far as that reason is disclosed in the incarnation, it is
to be equated with the sheer mystery of God's Love
which knows no reason beyond its own ultimateness as
the Love that God eternally is. Election refers to the
eternal decision which is nothing less than the Love
that God himself is, in action ; it is the unconditional
self-giving of God in the undeflecting constancy of his
Grace which, as we have seen, flows freely and equably
to all irrespective of any claim or worth or reaction on
their part.

In this perspective the doctrine of election is to be
appreciated as a way of expressing the unqualified
objectivity of God's Love and Grace toward us, and the
ultimate invariant ground in God himself on which all
our faith and trust in him for our salvation in life and
death repose. It represents a strictly theonomous way of
thinking, from a centre in God and not from a centre
in ourselves. As such the doctrine of election rejects any
idea that we may establish contact with God or know or
worship him through acting upon him, and certainly
any idea that we can induce God to act in accordance
with what we think or claim or want, for all our
relations with God derive from his activity in Grace
upon us whereby he freely establishes reciprocity
between himself and us, within which he makes room
for us and establishes us in an authentic creaturely
freedom grounded and secured in his own unlimited
Freedom as God. Thus the doctrine of election, as both
the Old Testament and the New Testament teach, is
the counterpart to the doctrine of the covenant of
Grace which God unilaterally establishes and maintains

between himself and his creation. The doctrine of
election also rejects any projection of human ways of
thought, speech or behaviour, or any creaturely
representation, into God — that is the way of mythology
— but calls instead for a radical discrimination of what
is objectively real in God from all our subjective states
and creaturely fancies. In this respect the doctrine of
election, as St. Paul made so clear, is the counterpart
to the doctrine of the incarnation as the projection of
God's eternal purpose of Love into our creaturely
existence and its embodiment in a unique and exclusive
way in Jesus Christ through whom true relations
between God and man and man and God are established. The incarnation, therefore, may be regarded as the
eternal decision or election of God in his Love not to be
confined, as it were, within himself alone, but to pour
himself out in unrestricted Love upon the world which
he has made and to actualise that Love in Jesus Christ
in such a way within the conditions of our spatio-
temporal existence that he constitutes the one Mediator
between God and man through whom we may all freely
participate in the unconditional Love and Grace of
God. Thus the incarnation was held by Reformed
theology, as it had been held by Patristic theology, to
be the exact antithesis of all mythology, for far from
being a projection of the human and the creaturely into
the realm of the divine, it is the self-projection of the
divine into the human which grounds all its creaturely
reality beyond itself in the objective Reality of God.

Now what became of this doctrine of election in
Protestant Scholasticism within the determinate yet
dualist framework of the Augustinian-Aristotelian
thought which it developed soon after the Reformation
and then of the Augustinian-Newtonian thought which
succeeded it? Reformed theology rightly stressed the
priority or prevenience or unsurpassability of God's

Grace and often preferred the term 'predestination' to
the term 'election', but what did it mean by the *pre* in
predestination? Originally it was intended to make the
point that the Grace by which we are saved is grounded
in the inner Life of God himself, and that we are saved
by the Grace of God alone. Predestination means
therefore that no matter what a man thinks or does he
cannot constitute himself a being under Grace, he
cannot constitute himself a man loved by God, for he is
that already. That is to say, the *pre* in predestination
emphasises the sheer objectivity of God's Grace.
However, a different view began to emerge in which
election could be spoken of as 'preceding grace', in line
with which predestination could be regarded as a
causal antecedent to our salvation in time. That is what
happened. Within the framework of Augustinian-
Aristotelian thought and its combination of St.
Augustine's notion of irresistible grace with an
Aristotelian doctrine of final cause, the concept of
predestination took on a strong determinist slant. And
within the framework of Augustinian-Newtonian
thought, in which absolute mathematical time and
space were clamped down upon relative phenomenal
time and space, causally and logically conditioning
them, the kind of *prius* with which, it was thought, we
operate in our temporal-spatial and logico-causal
connections was read back into divine predestination,
yet in an 'absolute' or 'inertial' way, so that there arose
the doctrine of so-called 'absolute particular predestination'. But to interpret *pre*-destination in this
way, as an absolute-temporal and absolute-causal
prius, gave rise to very grave problems.

On the one hand, it traced predestination back to an
eternal irresistible decree in God which by-passes, so to
speak, the incarnation and the cross, grounding it in
some arcane 'dark patch' in God behind the back of

Jesus Christ. This had the effect of driving a deep
wedge between Jesus Christ and God, thereby introduc-
ing by the back door an element of Nestorianism into
Calvinist Christology, which called in question any
final and essential relation between the incarnate Son
and God the Father and threatened to extinguish the
light of the Gospel. It is hardly surprising that a
Calvinism of this kind which stressed the utter impassibility and immutability of God should have given rise
again and again to a heretical liberal theology with its
denial of the Deity of Christ. Yet such a position is far
removed from that which Calvin himself adopted,
when he insisted that Christ himself is the 'mirror of
election', for it takes place *in him* in such a way that he
is the Origin and the End, the Agent and the Substance
of election—that is, if Aristotelian language is to be
used, Christ himself is to be thought of as the 'Cause' of
election in all four senses of 'cause', the formal and
final, the efficient and the material. Hence Calvin
insisted that to think of predestination as taking place
somehow apart from Christ is to plunge into an
inextricable 'labyrinth' of error and darkness.

On the other hand, by reading back (in some kind of
way) into God temporal, causal and logical relations
from our experience in this world, Calvinism was
forced to connect the relative apparent distinctions
between the believing and unbelieving, the obedient
and disobedient, to the absolute decree of God. Hence
predestination had to be construed (in the 'inertial' way
noted above) into the double form of 'election' and
'reprobation'. This entailed, however, a duality in God
himself, an ultimate 'Yes' and an ultimate 'No', which
could not be explained away by claiming, as was often
done, that the 'No' of reprobation was only a 'passing
over' of some people rather than a deliberate damnation
of them. At this point Calvinism is trapped in its own

logic. There is an important sense in which we may speak of 'the logic of grace', i.e., the pattern exhibited by God's Grace in the incarnation, life, death and resurrection of Christ, all through which he acted under the freely accepted constraint of his unreserved self-giving for our salvation. But to construe that in terms of necessary, logical connections is to convert grace into something quite other than it is, for it would imply, for example, that there is not a free contingent relation between the self-giving of Christ for us on the cross and our salvation, but a logico-causal relation. It is on the basis of just such a logico-causal understanding of divine Grace that the twin errors of 'limited atonement' and 'universal salvation' arise. Thus it is argued, *a posteriori*, that if as a matter of fact some people believe in Christ and are saved and others reject Christ and are damned, then Christ must have died only for the believing and not for the unbelieving. But it is also argued, *a priori*, that if Christ died for all people, then all people must be and will be saved. But of course if we had to depend on a logical relation between the death of Jesus and the forgiveness of our sins, we would all be unforgiven whether we believe or not.

Calvin himself had taken up a different position, in accordance with which he held with St. Paul that there is not a 'Yes' and a 'No' in God but only the 'Yes' of his Grace which he speaks equally to all, the just and the unjust alike. Hence if it happens that some people do not believe and perish, that can be understood only as an 'accidental' or 'adventitious' result, for Jesus Christ came to save and not to condemn, and it is of the nature of the Gospel to bring life and not death, just as it is the nature of light to enlighten and not bring blindness or darkness. That is to say, we cannot think this matter out on a logical basis, as if there has to be a kind of logical balance between election and reprobation, for in both the activity of God must be construed as Grace alone. It was for this reason that Calvin refused to agree that condemnation or reprobation should be inserted into a Christian confession of faith for it is an irrational and inexplicable happening, contrary to the intention of Christ and his Gospel.

Sufficient has been said to indicate that when the grace of election is submitted to interpretation within a dualist and determinate framework of thought governed by the primacy of number in which time and movement are transmuted into mathematical and mechanical patterns, the basic equilibrium of thought is disrupted and understanding of election ends up in contradictions and absurdities. Moreover, the concept of predestination with its stress upon the objectivity of Grace is turned on its head, for instead of being thought of as the dynamic self-movement of God's Love into our human existence in the incarnation of his eternal Son, it is distorted into a mythological projection into the realm of God's Being and Activity of culture-conditioned concepts and creaturely distinctions. Thus a radically objectivist notion of election or predestination passes over into its opposite.

(b) *'Christianity without incarnation'*. Here we are concerned with a way of thinking which is the very reverse of the Biblical understanding of election as the incarnational advent of God himself among men, in the unreserved self-giving of himself for their salvation, for it regards the incarnation as an extreme form of mythology in the projection of man and his worldly thought into the realm of the divine and therein an intolerable humanisation of the Deity. Here the all-significant theological equilibrium in the Biblical and Patristic understanding of Jesus Christ as God and man in one Person, the one Mediator between God and man, is disrupted, with the result that 'God' takes off, as it were, into an utterly transcendentalist realm, and man remains shut up within the realm of his own self-understanding, without any objective anchorage for his thought in the ultimate Reality and Truth of God. It should not surprise us, therefore, to find that the kind of thinking thrown up here from this side of the transcendentalist detachment of God from the world inevitably takes the form—no matter how much it is disguised—of an unalloyed mythological projection of man's own subjectivities into the Deity. Just as an arrow shot into the air invariably falls back to earth, so this way of thinking from a base in man's self-understanding, substituting his self-encounters for encounters with God, invariably converts theology into a form of anthropology, as Ludwig Feuerbach, Martin Buber and Karl Barth have all shown in their different ways. God is eclipsed from man by the intrusion of man himself between himself and God. Without entering into the details of this anachronistic resurgence today of nineteenth century thought, let us consider what has been happening by looking at it from the line of argument we have been developing about how Protestant theology took paradoxical shape within the framework of Augustinian-Newtonian thought.

The determinate structure of Newtonian science is not questioned but acknowledged as valid for scientific knowledge of what goes on in the universe, but it is understood according to the model of a rigid mechanical determinism which claimed and was allowed complete ascendancy in all rational knowledge. As such it automatically rules out of reckoning any conception of a divine or supernatural 'causality' within the closed causal nexus of nature, so that doctrines of incarnation or resurrection or of any information-laden act of divine revelation are discarded. At the same time the dualist basis on which this determinist view of the

universe rests, understood according to the Kantian
model of the radical dichotomy between a realm of
noumenal ideas or unknowable things-in-themselves
and a realm of knowable and quantifiable phenomenal
events, is readily accepted, for it appears to offer a way
of escape for the human spirit from the oppressive
tyranny of omnicompetent causality by making possible
two diverse and divergent interpretations of the same
events in our human experience, objective and non-
objective, determinate and indeterminate. So far as
theology is concerned this posits a yawning gap between
the other-worldly and the this-worldly, the divine and
the human, such that they bear upon one another only
in some tangential way at a timeless and vanishing
mathematical point. The effect of this is to rule out
entirely any idea of an interaction between God and
nature, or between divine agency and human agency in
history, and thereby to remove from knowledge of God
any objective or evidential ground and to empty faith
of any conceptual content of its own.

Thus while, on the one hand, the determinate
framework is accepted in deference to what is called the
scientific world-view, the epistemological dualism lying
behind it, on the other hand, is exploited in order to
develop an indeterminate framework which may be set
over against it, within which faith becomes a way of
thinking and seeking understanding from the non-
objective side of the dichotomy. From this point of view
in which God is thought of as utterly transcendent,
beyond the world and beyond all scientific thinking,
classical Christian doctrines like the incarnation or
atonement appear to be unwarranted this-worldly
objectifications which are mythologically projected on
to God, in an attempt to give the wholly other-worldly
activity of God a comforting this-worldly reality and
objectivity. As a matter of fact, of course, this

accusation of mythology levelled against Christian doctrine is itself the result of a severe refraction in thought brought about by the assumption of a radical dichotomy between the objectifiable and the non-objectifiable.

Clearly a 'theology' thrown up within such an indeterminate frame of reference (in which word-rationality is cut off from control by number-rationality) is sharply opposed to any form of rigorous or scientific theological thinking from an objective centre in the givenness of God, for it rejects from the very start any rational Word from God to man communicated within the created objectivities and intelligibilities of the space-time universe. Rather is this 'theology' itself a form of *mythological* thinking from an autonomous centre in the human self in which it projects anthropological ideas and patterns upon the divine Reality, since it will accept only what is conceivable in terms of man's own prior self-understanding. Quite consistently, therefore, Rudolf Bultmann used to claim 'The question of God and the question of myself are identical'. However, since knowledge of God alleged to arise in this way is essentially symbolic and indirect, or metaphorical and oblique, and *non-conceptual,* it must be rationalised through borrowing conceptuality from elsewhere if it is to have any acceptable place in human culture at all. Scientifically regarded, this way of thinking by retreat into the realm of the indeterminate, the mythical or the poetic, is particularly reactionary and obscurantist, for it detaches the basic knowledge of faith from the given fabric of empirical reality and disjoins it from all other objective rational structures of knowledge with reference to which it may be tested and purged of pseudo-scientific as well as pseudo-theological ideas and constructs.

This way of thinking which turns its back on the

objective ground which alone can give meaning to it, has a parallel in a development of modern science which we have already discussed. On the basis of the dualism posited by Galileo and Newton an extreme form of empiricism arose which passed over into a nominalistic formalism and conventionalism. In a one-sided emphasis upon the theoretical aspects of scientific knowledge, sequences and patterns of number were developed apart from their original objective reference into universal rational necessities, and then imposed prescriptively not so much upon nature itself as upon man's handling of nature but interpreted as convenient pragmatic arrangements with no claim to any bearing upon ontological structures in reality. However, as symbolic formalisations detached from reality they came to represent an inner world of physical experience and functioned as the carriers of a naturalistic outlook projected out of man's subjective fantasies but not derived from the objective intelligibilities of the universe. This naturalistic and secularistic development had the effect of emptying the world of meaning, but the dualist basis on which it rested, as we have seen, has been shattered by the profound transition in scientific understanding of the universe from Clerk Maxwell to Einstein. By the same token, however, the old dichotomy between determinate and indeterminate frames of thought is shattered as well, so that the regression of liberal theology today, whether of the Continental or Anglo-Saxon type, into a symbolic or mythical way of thinking of Christianity without incarnation has been blocked, at least so far as pure science is concerned.

There is another parallel to mythical thinking, however, still widespread in contemporary culture which we must note. This has to do with the now familiar search for one's proper image or identity which results from a schizoid malaise in modern life, namely, the detachment of image from reality in the roots of the human person and behind that the detachment of the human person from an objective ground in the creative Word and Rationality of God. Whenever image becomes detached from reality, it starts a free-floating life of its own and fails to touch down, and there results both a loss of identity which brings deep anxieties and a loss of rational control with the upsurge of fantasy. If the break between image and reality is severe a schizophrenic condition emerges in which nature spontaneously prompts a search for what Jung called 'mandalas', in an attempt to overcome the inner split through the unification of opposites or the collapse of polarities into 'the one'. We are familiar with this from Eastern religions, but where more than in the 'syzygies' of the Gnostic cults and their mythologies with which early Patristic theology had to contend? More usually, however, the relation between image and reality is damaged, when two things appear to happen. On the one hand, an ambiguous situation develops in which everything appears fuzzy and double-imaged, prompting diverse interpretations and the use of deceptive and prevaricating language. On the other hand, instead of being entirely cut loose the image is held in a tangential relation to reality, but as such it is without objective control and is a changeable image which chameleon-like constantly takes on the colours and forms of the changing environment. That was the charge, for example, which Athanasius and Hilary in the Early Church levelled against the Arian interpretation of 'the image of Christ', as detached from its Reality in God and as a changeable image subject to the fluctuations of human fancy and cultural change and as such projected into 'the Son of God'. Basically it is the same issue at stake today between a Christology which takes its cue from the Nicene Creed and its modern 'Arian' critics.

Now it would seem that a schizoid malaise of this kind can affect a whole culture. Thus it is possible for a culture, uprooted from consistent structures of objective rationality, to suffer from a widespread alienation of meaning, and to flounder about looking for its proper image or identity. Or it can affect a whole period of human thought when a damaging split opens up between inner and outer worlds, language and reality, or form and content, and a highly symbolic or mythical way of thinking takes over in which the prevailing images of thought are not used for their objective reference but as ways of expressing the human self in its search for identity and meaning. That would seem to be the state of affairs in modern Western culture with its deep split between the sciences and the humanities and a general disintegration of form in the arts, in which the phenomenon of modern liberal theology with its revival of mythical thinking is rooted.

If this is the case, as I believe it to be, it would be quite pointless to speak to the problems of liberal theology at the surface level of its symbolic structures which are clearly the carriers of deep-set anxieties and fantasies. Rather must this kind of thinking be taken back to the damaging dichotomy between the determinate and indeterminate in its foundations, and given a new reference to the unitary understanding of reality that has been opened up in our scientific culture through the revolution in the foundations of knowledge which we have been discussing in this book. What is required by all modern theology is a profounder equilibration in its understanding of the incarnation and the creation and in the understanding of theological science and natural science. And to that I believe rigorous natural science, operating with its profound integration of physical and intelligible ingredients in nature and in our knowledge of it, has a great deal to contribute. As Walter R. Thorson, the Canadian theoretical chemist, has been insisting in a number of recent publications, there is a spiritual authenticity to natural science which Christians must not ignore, for it is grounded in the authenticity — the genuine depth and integrity — of the creation as it came from God. Hence he says: 'I think that the scientific revolution and the new kind of thinking it encourages should properly be understood as a new expression of Christian thought, and not as an irrelevant and divergent secularism'. What it does do, is to point us back behind the various dualisms which have been afflicting our human life and thought to a deeper appreciation of the consistent structure and integrity of the material world, and indeed to the objective Rationality of God, without reference to which the natural world and human existence, not to speak of theology itself, are progressively emptied of significance.

BOOKS RELEVANT TO THIS CHAPTER

KARL BARTH.
Church Dogmatics, II.1. T and T Clark, Edinburgh, 1958.

G. W. BROMILEY.
Introduction to the Theology of Karl Barth. T and T Clark, Edinburgh, 1980.

R. BULTMANN.
Jesus Christ and Mythology. Charles Scribner's Sons, New York, 1958.

J. HICK (Editor).
The Myth of God Incarnate. SCM, London, 1977.

E. L. MASCALL.
Christian Theology and Natural Science. Longmans Green, London, 1956.
Theology and the Gospel of Christ. An Essay in Reorientation. SPCK, London, 1977.

D. ALEXANDER.
Beyond Science. A. J. Holman, Philadelphia and New York, 1972.

E. H. HUTTEN.
The Origins of Science. An Inquiry into the Foundations of Western Thought. Allen and Unwin, London, 1962.

W. R. THORSON.
'The Spiritual Dimensions of Science', in *Horizons of Science.* Ed. by C. F. H. Henry. Harper & Row, New York, 1978.

R. SCHLEGEL.
Superimposition and Interaction. Chicago University Press, Chicago, 1980.

T. F. TORRANCE.
Theology in Reconstruction. SCM Press, London, 1965.
God and Rationality. Oxford University Press, London, 1971.
Divine and Contingent Order. Oxford University Press, New York, 1981.

INDEX OF PERSONS

INDEX OF SUBJECTS